HOW TO
KILL
POETRY

raymondluczak.com

HOW TO KILL POETRY

Raymond Luczak

SIBLING RIVALRY PRESS
Alexander, AR

How to Kill Poetry.

Cover design by Mona Z. Kraculdy. For a detailed listing of acknowledgments and image credits, please see page 108.

Sibling Rivalry Press, LLC
13913 Magnolia Glen Drive
Alexander, AR 72002

siblingrivalrypress.com
info@siblingrivalrypress.com

ISBN: 978-1-937420-29-1
Library of Congress Control Number: 2012948878

First Sibling Rivalry Press Edition, March 2013

FOR
BRYAN BORLAND

CONTENTS

Thus Spake Zarathustra: 30,000 BCE to 2013 CE

The Warmth of Winter: 2213 CE

Leaves of Glass: 2363 CE

Thus Spake Zarathustra

30,000 BCE *to* 2013 CE

"Every body writes poetry, and yet there is not a single poet."
— Walt Whitman

THE FIRST POEMS

In the beginning no one spoke :

Like babies who try to communicate first
not with voices but with their hands ,
our first ancestors gestured : our first language .

[Touch-nose move-circles-air
Touch-nose move-circles-there   *what wafts everywhere : you*
Touch-nose move-circles-here
Touch-nose-you]

Then came nights of silence and explosions of sound
from afar at dawn .

grunt-grunt-grunt [finger-closed lips]   *animal nearby : all quiet*
   [fingersnaps]
grunt Grunt GRUNT [chest-slap] grunt   *animal there billowing its chest*
grunt Grunt GRUNT [chest-slap] grunt   *animal over there billowing its chest*
grunt GRUNT GRUNT GRUNT [slap-slap]   *animals together clash-clash-clash*
   TA !   *DEATH*

Then came days when mothers breastfed their babies .
They were our first songwriters .

Ma-ma-ma-ma-*mmm*-ma   *you, you, you are my milk*
Ma-ma-ma-ma-MMM-ma   *you, you, you are my baby*

Then came the first Poet , full of I ,
much like the Ancient of Days
full of thunderclaps splitting
the walnut shells of their brains
into quaking jelly halves :

BA BA BA BA BA *BA* !   *I am here — listen to me*

"Taxation is transactional and not cuneiform. Our tax laws are not so supple that scraps of paper, regardless of their callifgraphy, can transmute trade-ins into sales. Although Redwing's transfers may have been paper sales, they were actual exchanges." — Redwing Carriers, Inc. and Rockana Carriers, Inc., v. Laurie W. Tomlinson, former Director of Internal Revenue for the District of Florida, US-CT-APP-5 (August 22, 1968)

CUNEIFORMS

The first writer used a chisel and hammer
to make her point in clay.
Crumbs and pebbles fell away from the tablet.
"This here," she said, "means *You own this many
bushels of grain and fish.*
This means *Your children will own this land
after you die.* This power means
*Everyone needs to memorize the shapes,
the lines, this very occasion.*"

Centuries passed. Lines became smaller,
dense with grammar and meaning.
Entire lives were written in a single sentence
in stones that no one can entirely decipher.
Linguists have tried. It is the one language
miraculously out of nowhere:
no ancestors, no lineage to trace
the evolution of original thought.

Its chiseled marks catch sun and shadow,
the only language that hasn't changed.
The only definite translation is *Witness.*

OF PAPYRUS, REBORN
after Sappho (approximately 630 BCE – 570 BCE)

Centuries of wandering as a ghost
has given me an ear for things.

When I was a young woman
famed for singing and playing my lyre,
a small group of learned men in Athens
asked me to repeat each line.

I watched them write on rolls of papyrus.
I couldn't believe my words
looked like that. So mysterious.
They looked like veins ready to splay.

These married men looked at me
with intense longing. I was just a woman
with a lyre. I had a husband and a daughter,
but all that was expected of me.

The incompleteness of those fragments,
torn asunder from carelessness and time,
is what keeps everyone coming back, filling
in the gaps of what must be, who I am.

For centuries I listened to people
far more learned than those men in Athens
argue that I couldn't be like those women
named after the island I so loved.

There are too many sad songs.
It pains to play my lyre. Silence is easier.

HELEN OF TROY

Homer was first to spread my legend,
proclaiming my beauty justified
as the mere cause for war.
For ten years, soldiers died.

I hid my face behind a veil
when men never knowing me
gave up their lives and whispered
their last words: "My Helen!"

A few wives lunged knives at me.
Their men had fallen for me.
Nights of encampment they swore
nothing else but of their victory:

He would be the one to show me
how deeply wronged I'd been.
He would bed me in a temple,
just reward for his years of faith.

Words of my beauty trickled back.
I am short. I am tall. I am flawless.
I am long-haired. I am short-haired.
I have no wrinkles. I have perfect skin.

But what these men never knew:
I had a huge splotchy mole
just above my pubic hairs
and cellulite padding my thighs.

I was happier when my body started
to sag from age. Men scattered
when they saw my double chins.
Damn you, Homer, and your lies.

INCUNABULUM

❡ 1. Everything, including the Bible, was copied by hand. Each book was as unique as its letterers, and frightfully expensive. Ink and blood were of the same consistency. Stiff wrists and sore shoulders were of no consequence. ❡ 2. His first bestseller, which sold 180 copies for a clerk's three years of wages, didn't bear his likeness. There was no editor's bio. Johannes Gutenberg, a goldsmith and inventor, had simply wanted to make money off his printing press, using movable type alloyed of lead, tin, and antimony. Compared to the cumbersome woodblock printing, movable type was lightning. ❡ 3. Each page of the Bible had 42 lines, filling up with words that suddenly looked uniform and lined up like soldiers ready for inspection. Priests no longer had to rely on memory and handwritten copies. Parishioners gazed upon these new Bibles with wonder. How was it possible that each page could look the same and within margins? The illustrations drawn by hand varied from copy to copy, but the word and the Word, entwined like twins, whispered a quiet authority. This here was a miracle of God. ❡ 4. As printing books became cheaper and easier, the hunger for literacy spread like a slow-burning virus. People, particularly women who were made to feel unequal to men, died of it. Nothing could save them. The idea of educating the serfs, those who worked the land and served the privileged, was pure pox. ❡ 5. Infections soon became commonplace. Each teacher became a doctor, prescribing Latin, and determined what their written language and penmanship should look like. Each patient begged the sweet morphine of words leeching all over their bodies. Imagination was the elixir, the true fountain of youth. ❡ 6. Today some people resist the anesthesia of modernity when they hunt for incunabulum (after *prima typographicae incunabula*, "the first infancy of printing," or anything that was printed, not handwritten, before the year 1501 in Europe). They wear white cotton gloves as if to slice open the fragile body there before them under the architect's magnifying lamp. Sometimes, when they think no one's looking, they drop their noses a few centimeters above the dust of time and inhale, imagining themselves in places and among people forever nameless. ❡ 7. Away from the day's chores and in the evening shadows by candlelight in the fading days of the fifteenth century, some of these outpatients began to scribble, performing the weird alchemy of ink, word, and paper to produce gold of the highest carat. The element of each word was weighed carefully before pronounced worthy of trade and print. The more one wrote, the more one forgot about centuries of the ear listening. The poem began to weaken, sicker without the drug of listening. No one noticed. The poem was simply propped up on the pillow and given a mixture of medicinal herbs. These days it is a breathing corpse. ❡❡ Ah, the ear, the ear! What the Lord giveth, and what the Lord taketh away.

"The firm desire that enters
Can neither be taken from my heart by beak or nail . . ."
— Arnaut Daniel, as translated by Craig E. Bertolet

JUST ANOTHER TROUBADOUR
after Benart de Ventadorn (approximately 1125 - 1190)

The road is long, lined with tales I've yet to tell,
but seeing you makes me forget the hell

I've endured coming back. In your window
you sit pretty as if you're my patron.
Forgive me while I fiddle my weapon.
Please don't look away if my voice strains so.

This bow is my choir, voicing all your dreams.
Close your eyes. Everything will be what seems.

My days are weary, filled with starvation.
Yet I'll stand right here, perfecting each note
'til my one love song is no longer rote:
None compares to you, my heart's salvation.

Go ahead, laugh. Cast me aside again.
When you're old and fat, you'll pine for me then.

THE RICHNESS OF SPIT
after William Shakespeare (1564 - 1616)

I.

It was the golden age of cross-dressing. Women weren't allowed to act onstage, so actors dressed up in dresses, shawls, and frilly gloves. Everyone in the audience knew this, so it was always good for a laugh, especially when a man wore a different dress the next time he returned.

2.

From behind the curtain Mr. Shakespeare watched the actor Richard Burbage go through his motions on the creaky pull-stage. How that man could easily make everyone chuckle and laugh with a single bat of his eye!

3.

The iambic pentameter controls speech much like indentations of land with water where it should go. Rhyme no longer has reason to irrigate.

4.

No record exists of whether Mr. Shakespeare ever wore a dress onstage and gave a chaste kiss to Mr. Burbage. Speculation is what drives audiences to come see the truth for themselves. What's laughable is their gullibility: what truly matters is not what happens onstage but behind closed doors. For all we know, Mr. Shakespeare decoyed all.

5.

In those days no one was a director. Memorizing, memorizing. Ah, the lines! That darn snake-snarl of words again. Actors spoke the language of those who flocked to their shows. How strange and repulsive our modern English, remade in that television-standardized accent, would sound to their ears!

They would stand there, disbelieving that we of highfalutin education could render their memories into illegibility in the name of "authenticity." No richness of spit, no bump-that-elbow chuckle at the undercurrent of pun, no acknowledgment of the bawdy filth the actors spoke backstage. All that memorizing for not even a slap-your-thigh gut belly laugh?

6.

He listened without judgment. That was *the* secret to his writing. His ears told him all he needed to tell his actors what to say. That, and the constant reading of precious books helped.

7.

Scholars world over would die to see the original copy of the plays he wrote. Copies in his own hand do not exist. No such thing as mimeograph or photocopy in those days. Memory and repetition were the only job security for these actors. Speak, time your entrances well, or die!

Rumors of faking his talent in these 37 plays still persist. Hesitations and debates thrive in such a cottage industry. Queen Elizabeth I and James I are no longer around to order executions on the sly, so all's fair in love and war.

Mud is constantly slung in these ivory-white towers, so much that these splotches of mole-brown wet on the wall become considered as "art" and "valid statements" if only to avoid the unseemly task of cleaning these walls. The honesty of whiteness becomes a critical derision.

8.

He lay there not thinking of his wife Anne or the children he'd sired with her but the fair youth for whom he'd poured himself into these strict fourteen lines with tenderness and ache. Words and meaning rolled around like a ship amidst an angry sea of want on his tongue. No, he would never tell a single soul his name nor tell the fair youth for he couldn't read anyway. It would be centuries before a cheeky fellow named Oscar Wilde decoded his secret.

9.

When he was young, ale was all he had some nights in the pub. Small talk was mere appetizers to a meal that he couldn't afford. The crackle of fire lulled him into sleep. Sometimes if he stayed close enough, it would be loud enough to mask the roar of hunger.

He shut the spoiled child's needling of his stomach and opened up the mouth of his brain, playing around with entire lines before he set them forth on paper. Never enough paper; they were expensive. Ink and quills too. Careful, careful, he always had to be.

No one thought about calories or the amount of fat sizzling there in a cast iron kettle. Just ate whatever possible. Never knew sometimes where their next meal came from.

10.

Sometimes the writing got tiring. Who cared about what Hamlet thought? Or that silly-head Juliet?

Writing the history plays were the hardest, trying to kiss the royal ass. The only way he could endure those mind-numbing stories was to play with the language, make it sing a bit more than before. Sometimes he rewrote lines to affect the rhythms of folk songs he'd heard out on the road. Ah, music!

Anyone who could play a music instrument was a rich man in poor people's eyes. How sweet it was to hear something orderly yet emotional after a day of dung and sod. Music was the key to all their dreams. All they had to do was to clap and sing when the fiddler strummed away.

11.

Everyone wanted to be next to Mr. Burbage once the show was over. It didn't matter if they had to strike the set, roll things up, and stuff it onto the lanky cart for the next leg of their tour. Mr. Burbage was always full of high spirits once ale entered his blood. Memories of mimicking people he knew while growing up came to the fore once he saw he had a ready-made audience. Laughs bounced off the beams and walls. He never noticed Mr. Shakespeare staring intently at him from a dark corner, not knowing how much Mr. Shakespeare wanted that gift of charisma and mimicry.

12.

Walking the long and ponderous road from one town to another, the actors memorized their lines, often improving on their rhythms. Their sole copy of these plays transcribed by hand was their most precious hymnbook.

The first time Mr. Shakespeare heard them butcher his lines when they returned to the Globe, he was furious. But once the fury faded away like embers of a campfire, he listened as if he'd never heard them before. By God, they had improved on his writing. They made him sound better!

It was all about the bloody ear.

13.

Late at night Mr. Shakespeare's bones in his crypt still rattle, no blood left in the marrow. Footsteps after centuries of wonder and worship are like injections of blood. No one cares about Mr. Burbage or Ms. Hathaway or any of the people who acted with him onstage anymore. He knows history's lost all track of him except these new and improved lines. Just a name now loaded with meaning in the death of classrooms.

Back then his name meant that he was a shrewd businessman who happened to write what audiences wanted to hear. He was envied for all that money! He no longer cared about the art. He was too tired, more interested in earning even more now that Mr. Burbage was gone, a legend among those who knew him. No one cared about Mr. Shakespeare as a person; he was actually quite boring, his creative ambition dried out of him. He was all money and land now.

If alive, Mr. Shakespeare would roll his eyes and shake his head at the numerous fictions and legends concocted out of the few incontestable facts about his life. Including my own lame attempt to re-imagine him as something that he probably never was.

He'd cock his head and peer into my eyes. I wouldn't be able to understand his accent thick with the dust of centuries. But from poet to poet, I would sense what he'd say should he master today's bewildering English: "Rubbish. No music your poetry are. At all!"

14.

Everybody used to want to be the next Shakespeare, but no, all the fair youths want to be the next hot filmmaker. It's all about the connections, the deals, the distribution, the constant media saturation, the buzz.

Romance, an artificial device reconstructed to fill more theater seats, is now a middle-fingered sonnet.

THE OTHER SKIN

after Phillis Wheatley (1753? – 1784), the first African-American poet

She never knew color had to matter so much.
But on the slave ship westward to Boston,
in that stark vastness of ocean and nothingness,
she learned to fear the color of pale peach,
easily sunburned and freckled. Two years
later, at the age of nine, she was sold as a servant
for Master Wheatley's wife Susanna in Boston.
She was fortunate her masters were progressive
enough to tutor her in reading and writing.
By the time she turned twelve,
she could read Greek and Latin classics.
She wasn't just another domestic slave anymore.
The other slaves in her household resented
how she was almost treated as their betters.
She was shown off to Master Wheatley's
friends and family. But the ghosts
of dead men whispered poetry into her ear.
Writing original thoughts in verse, she sensed,
would be an act of infamy against those
who demanded to keep every slave in shackles.
She couldn't remember much from her homeland,
but she knew to lie. She praised the men
who brought her to the cause of Christianity:
"Remember, Christians, Negroes, black as Cain,
May be refin'd, and join th' angelic train."
Readers found the notion of a slave poet like her
impossible. She had to defend herself,
her very act of authorship, in court.
White learned men questioned her to no end
until they signed an attestation to her abilities.
No one in Boston wanted to publish her book,
but a publisher in London did. Praising
the sun, an echo from her days in Senegal,
remembering her parents worshipping
that pale face that bestowed miracles on them

in the days before they were kidnapped,
she wanted to disrobe herself
of the white togas her literary masters wore
and unzip herself of the dark skin
that had so long singled her out
for a skin of no color where no one
would notice. Like Homer,
everyone would be blind and only hear
her, a spirit yearning to shimmer like Christ.

O VISIONS!
after William Blake (1757 – 1827)

I.

On the grassy slope, lambs climbed
And fell into a tumbling,
Their eyes wide as day at noontime
Awaiting their mothering.

With the winds pushing her,
A sweet-dimpled girl sat on a swing
And giggled for another
Round of the nearby world bobbing.

Above the girl stood angels quiet
With their wings glowing,
Their rustle in the leaves a sight
For lambs still playing.

2.

You were very young when you had visions.
God rested His head on the windowsill.
Angels appeared in your tree one day.
They never left your side when you drew.

You learned to illuminate such words,
Whispers in the ear of your dreams.
Your pencil sang hymns while you starved.
You were too intense for ordinary patrons.

You drew and printed what you saw and heard.
Angels and devils were full of supple and sinew.
You died poor and unrecognized.
Today you'd be force-fed psychotropic drugs.

3.

Come cloak me in the choke of smoke
Unfurling out of the chimneys
Plugged with children small enough
To scale bricks to sweep clean.

Come pull away the curtain of uncertainty,
The first glare of sun in my eyes,
My pale skin defenseless against the ultraviolet
Lava ready to pour from hell's cauldron.

Come gift my beastly back with wings
So I may fly with you and sing
Rosy-cheeked cherubs and lambs
Playing tag in the meadows of innocence.

I haven't lived enough poetry.
O angels! O demons! O visions!

I WAS ELVIS BEFORE ELVIS WAS ELVIS
after George Gordon Byron, otherwise known as Lord Byron (1788 – 1824)

I was born with a clubfoot. I tried
all sorts of things to fix it, hide it.
My relatives drank, cheated, escaped debts,
and indulged in incest. Like my father,
when I came into inheritance at age ten
after too many relatives in line
died one after another, I was gifted
with the glow of charisma and wealth,
a grandiose vision of oneself without defect.
I *had* to have certain things: books,
clothes, horses, and carriages.
I didn't care if there were enough funds.
It helped that I hated my mother,
an uneducated woman who didn't know
how to carry herself in high society.
I swore never to see her again so off I went
to far-off lands away from England. For two years
I saw so much that I wrote *Childe Harold's
Pilgrimage* about a poet so bored that he went
in search of adventure. The book caused
such a sensation in London that women swooned
in public. They believed that I was as debonair,
adaptable to new situations, and helpless
around fair maidens. Instead I was full of conceit
and contempt for my bastard children.
Then *Don Juan* came out. Readers were shocked
by its "immoral content." I didn't care.
I slept with one man and woman after another.
I picked up a few venereal diseases along the way.
Even when I recovered, I still stayed in love
with the idea of Love, a-twitter like sparrows
hopping about until the winter of contentedness
bored me until I saw a new glorious spring

in the eyes of another. Taboo was even hotter
in the arms of my half-sister, my lover-to-be
my father had conceived with another woman.
My wife hated hearing us moaning upstairs.
But how I adored my Augusta! She was my flame.
The whispers of scandal followed me everywhere.
Divorce money had to be quietly negotiated.
I had to get out of England. I traveled Europe.
The older I became, the less *Don Juan* I became.
I had to work harder to make people love me.
My teeth had become discolored; my hair, graying.
I instructed painters never to show me with a book,
a pen, or paper. I didn't want to look like a dullard
pump-breasted with pomp. I had to stay forever young.
Today, if I were alive, I'd be a rock star
making sure to die at the plucky age of 27
and inspire a whole wave of cult disciples
willing to overlook my drug-addled assholism
for my genius at living art so recklessly.
Who knew debauchery could be so respectable?

> "Everybody here is so like everybody else—and I am
> Walt Whitman!" — Walt Whitman

AMERICA'S FIRST COMING OUT
after Walt Whitman (1819 – 1892)

Once I pass'd through a populous city . . .
with its shows, architecture, customs, and traditions.
You roamed the lower Broadway in the 1840s, didn't you,
looking for the errant eye of a handsome young rogue
in need of a drink and a bedding-down.
No one needed to know. Marriage was for nellies.
We two boys together clinging, One the other never leaving.
You allowed yourself to be sunburnt and freckled.
You were already gray by the time you turned thirty.
You were already a daddy in training.

Then in 1848, you went down to New Orleans.
I remember only the man who wandered with me,
there, for love of me. Your senses
must've exploded in such sensuous love
of his tongue on yours, how sweet the soil
upon which he stood before you. Revelations
of sight, smell, taste, sound, and touch
couldn't be hidden inside your breast pocket.
You have given me love! therefore I to you give love!
O unspeakable passionate love!
You had to sing like Marietta Alboni, damn them all!

Life, the greatest opera on earth, unleashed
in you lines, garrulous and rambling,
one after another, celebrating not just him
whose name we shall never know
but all whom you'd loved down on the docks,
the upper echelons of Astor Place Opera House,
and lower Broadway. *Again he holds me by the hand—I must not go!*
Everywhere was a possibility of conjugation
between men, women, and all capable of living.
How could anyone *not* see such music? *I hear America singing.*

"How I wish you were mine, as you once were, when I had you in the morning, and when the sun went down, and was sure I should never go to sleep without a moment from you." — from a letter by Emily Dickinson to Jane Humphrey, a former schoolmate

SNOW-LIGHT

after Emily Dickinson (1830 – 1886)

Winter chained me — Drafts —
Who galloped pages — Footprints white —
Flames of secrets — Walls snaked —
My hair auburn — Girl so slight —

Away from home — Lost in books —
Floor stone-cold — Stars ghosting night —
No fireplace — Puffs of dreams —
We clung — Dawn-light —

No one had names — What we did —
We folded secrets — The Quilt —
Now wear I white — Full of Blemishes —
Bride in absentia — Snow-Light

TEN SUREFIRE STEPS TO BECOME A BAD VICTORIAN POET
Or, How to become the next Henry Wadsworth Longfellow (1807 – 1882)

1. Read a number of turgid poems, usually long in the tooth about nothing, while in school, when you haven't done a lot of reading. Teething isn't required in bad poetry. Listen to your teacher drone on and on how great the boring and maundering poem at hand is. Daydream how much better you can write than that long-bearded nimbus fellow Longfellow. If he can earn up to three thousand dollars per poem (as for his "Hanging of the Crane"), why—of course, so can you! (To be considered a great poet of the age, be sure to include your middle name in your byline. Middle initials simply won't do.)

2. With each new masterpiece, finger-count each syllable and think of each tap a coin filling your till. The more words you stuff in a line, the richer your potential becomes!

3. Write your first love poem filled with adolescent clichés, only that you don't know they are. (The less you read, the less you analyze what you read by the greats, the worse you will become at your craft. It's even better to reread your brilliant poems obsessively and never making a correction. This point can't be emphasized enough.)

4. When the object of your affections rebuffs you, beseech her with a frilly poem twice as long saying the same thing as the first. As long as you compare her to a rose yet to peak with its sweet fragrances wafting on a spring wind, she shall bestow before you and offer her dainty hand in marriage. Poetic ardor is the best aphrodisiac.

5. Stand in front of the mirror in all your Sunday finery and perfect the sonorous rhythms of your lines. Each word must have equal weight. Be so totally in love with the timbre of your voice. When you start to use more and more exclamation points, perfect the art of shaking your fist at the air while spitting out each syllable with such force that people in the front row must use doily handkerchiefs to wipe their faces.

6. Allow your ego to swell, and swell even more, when your mother claps with glee in the parlor room. Truly wonderful! Amazing! Genius! Ignore the sound of others clapping weakly.

7. Listen to your pastor remarking on the agility of your wit and deep insights. Take his encouragement to write religiously wretched poems to heart. You cannot stop writing. Your exalted genius is your meal ticket to Heaven!

8. Post a few poems to the London *Times*, or any other newspaper that encourages sanctimonious verse. Soon enough you see your name in print. Your neighbors compliment you. Never mind the fact that they're illiterate; only that they'd heard the news from others. Fame and fortune are, by God, all yours for the taking!

9. Send off a sheaf of meticulously hand-copied poems to a publisher in Boston or thereabouts. Be humble in your cover letter. Be sure to mention your pastor's name. When the publisher finally offers you a contract, make ecstatic love to your comely mistress and then show an endearing humility when you break the news of your first book contract to your lard-assed wife.

10. Look for another mistress when your first one doesn't appreciate your genius with each collection of verse until you become impotent with clichéd rhymes. Die without ever knowing that your work, particularly the one listing a lady's rainbow of succulent aromas on a bright summer day rising above the stench-wafted Thames, would be included in tongue-in-cheek anthologies celebrating the very worst of bad poetry.

"I'm now making myself as scummy as I can. Why? I want to be a poet, and I'm working at turning myself into a seer. You won't understand any of this, and I'm almost incapable of explaining it to you. The idea is to reach the unknown by the derangement of all the senses. It involves enormous suffering, but one must be strong and be a born poet. It's really not my fault." — Arthur Rimbaud, as translated by Graham Robb

CONVULSIONS
after Arthur Rimbaud (1854 – 1891)

The first lesson a poet learns is to see everything as is.

The second is how important it is to lie.

There in the arms of my stoic sister trying to endure my screams of agony is not Isabelle herself but the flickers of halo and shadow on the wall behind her. I am a candle melting in a cauldron of wax.

The tiny claws of my fingers are stronger than meat hooks. I am a spirit borne of absinthe and hashish, spewing maggots and dripping crimson in the butchery. I'm not a symbol in search of a meaning.

I wrote poems celebrating the pungent pucker.

Only when I can offend you deeply as possible will I know how much I've mattered to you.

The love of my life, the only one who'd truly understood me, leaned forward and opened like a flower in the final seconds before I crushed its petals in the wrinkled folds of my hands.

He wanted more derangement. I punctured him with tiny pricks of knife until he tried to shoot me and went mad in prison for God, the god who'd inspired Satan to whisper his red-hot tinnitus dares in my groin's ear.

Only disciplines of Lucifer would understand my little bible of illuminations. I had to disappear like Jesus.

My feet didn't want home no matter where I stayed. Then my right leg got amputated. I couldn't sleep for days. The pain, the paranoia, the phantom limb.

My shiny horns that proclaimed my innate evilness on the streets of Paris had been long worn down in the heat of Abyssinia.

I was a moneymaker who'd mastered the language of money no matter what dialect the tribesmen spoke.

Camels can survive seven days without water. Their humps, made of fat, can sustain them for three weeks. Their feces are so dry they can fuel fire.

Late at night they rest and listen to nomads tattooed from the sun and bundled in layers talk in low voices under the stars crystalline as ice.

The first snap of cold is always a homecoming, but not this time.

I am just another dying lunatic in a hospital in Marseilles. My body is a desert, hot and wan and flush with stabs of pain.

Deep enough is the fur coat of cold, and deeper is the belly of hyperthermia, filled with floes of ice.

The needle prick of tongue is where the geyser of pus erupts, breaking the parched skin into the malaria of desire.

NO IS YES AND YES IS NO

after Gertrude Stein (1872 - 1946)

A poem is not a poem may be a poem.
My hands are but a single line.
Listen not what I say but what they do.
Bang dum dum. Who. Now.
They scribble words unspooling
a skein scrambled in the squiggles
of brain, memory, books.
This here a word not needed.
Watch sighs bounce in winds.
Summer days, winter seasons.
Alone words break backs.
Sit quiet. Birds flick.
I know you or you know I.
Sense makes nothing.
Woman is man of the world.
Gardens explode buttons.
Forever too short a fuse.

MS. MONROE'S REBUTTALS

after Harriet Monroe (1860 – 1936), the founding editor of Poetry

Hewn out of sestinas,
    I'm a woman informed
of the to-and-fro talk
    between the old and new,
quill-pens and typewriters.
    No more nice-looking words.[1]

I couldn't stand more birds
    twittering sestinas.
Victorian writers
    had to adhere to form
and rhyme, just to make do?
    No more overwrought talk![2]

Where was that spritely talk,
    the same I'd always heard
when I mingled among new
    artists and ballerinas
ready to weather storms?
    No more stuffy writers.[3]

In my mailbox writers
    sometimes made humble talk
and showed their work in form.
    Some felt like idle words;
some, mawkish sestinas.
    No more roses red, blue.[4]

But came along a few
    who made me love writers
despite their sestinas.
    They caused a lot of talk
and quite some angry words.
    No more corsets of form.[5]

[1] "The average magazine editor's conception of good verse is verse that will fill out a page. No editor is looking for long poems; he wants something light and convenient. Consequently a Milton might be living in Chicago today and be unable to find an outlet for his verse."

[2] "Another reason was the common desecration of the art by prosy teachers in schools and colleges, and the cheaply melodramatic presentation of poor specimens by 'elocutionists' on club platforms and elsewhere."

[3] "There were plenty of pessimists to predict a worthless assemblage of petty rhymesters under soft feminine editorship, and to size up unfavorably even the better-known poets of a rather sterile period . . . It was a gamble, with a risk always in any venture, so why not play for a high stake, and place my wager on the poets of the coming era?"

[4] "Either these pictures are good or they are not. If they are good, they will make their way in spite of objections; if not, they will perish without the aid of objections."

[5] "In a profound sense these radical artists are right. They represent the revolt of the imagination against nineteenth-century realism; they represent disgust with the camera, outrage over superficial smoothness which covers up weakness of structure. They represent a search for new beauty, impatience with formulae, a reaching out toward the inexpressible, a longing for new versions of truth."

I had to write; inform-
    ing men, all flustered blue,
why I'd published such words.
    I welcomed new writers,
new eras, and new talk.
    No more dull sestinas![6]

[6] 'Miss Monroe led us to suppose she was building a cathedral—it now appears that it was a Woolworth Building,' says one critic. A cathedral, did I? Modern cathedrals are second-rate—mere imitations. I would rather build a first-rate skyscraper!"

Writers are our best architects. They form
dream-like blueprints to provoke thought and talk.
All live and die by fine-tuned words: sestinas.

THE IMAGISTE
after Ezra Pound (1885 – 1972)

I am a devil's bastard from Hailey, Idaho.
My tongue's a Babel's spitfire.

Moralizing is bad for my appetite.
The Victorians sooted too many veils.

Too much babble, too much nothing.
Language is a huge chunk of marble.

Our hands must sculpt the ethereal.
Inhale the dust and exhale the music.

My voice is an instrument of the gods.
Fascism is good for the soul.

I am loyal to treason against the false.
Asylum's even better. I am a canto.

Confucius whispers constantly in my ear.
Strip, strip away. My brain's on fire.

YOU REAL COOL
after Gwendolyn Brooks (1917 – 2000)

No more listening to those men
who'd studied and became so learned
they turned blind to your color,
insisting the classics, created by men
they themselves considered worthy,
were the only stories that mattered.
They held themselves in high regard
like the Greek gods of literature
and philosophy. They peered at you
through their horn-rimmed glasses
and gave you tight little smiles.
Imagine their collective shock of surprise
when a few enlightened souls awarded
your second book the Pulitzer Prize.
You were officially in. The fact
that you were the first black writer
to win hung like vestments on your chest.
You were the new priestess, rising
higher than Langston Hughes
and others of the Harlem Renaissance.
But you *had* to know how deep
the white distrust of you and your kind ran.
You had to have felt the collective joy of defiance
when Rosa Parks didn't give up her seat
on the bus. Then the Little Rock Nine—
their ordeal had to have gripped your heart
so tightly that you must've only whispered.
The picket signs on fuzzy television screens
were poems with blades more incisive
than carefully-wrought iambic pentameter.
Your words among theirs were the cannonballs
blasting the canon of bland whiteness
to pieces until you became anthologized,
embalmed in the same crypt of dead white gods.

SIX GALLERY, SAN FRANCISCO: 7 OCTOBER 1955
on the first time Allen Ginsberg (1926 – 1997) reads "Howl" in public

Fog from down the bay unfurled its mystic kisses from deep inside America yet to be plumbed and renamed, only to find itself pressed against the glass windows, already fragile from the constant bombing of words and lines by the six poets swearing to take on the world of academic and elitist poetry. Claps flitted around the tiny gallery after each poem uttered, no longer a dream but a reality anchoring and climbing inside the listener's ear. Then came the fifth poet, all shaven and bespectacled not yet full of Jack Kerouac's "first thought, best thought" writing philosophy that would later render him downright impotent some three decades later, but there he was, drunk from cheap wine with a sheaf of typewritten papers, check-marked with constant corrections and deletions and reinsertions. As he lumbered through his poem for Carl Solomon, the train-clanging lines that once seemed like whispers in his own dreams began to eject powerful gusts of steam, he couldn't stop, he was finally waking up, the words were smooth as glass down the rail of mountains bye-bye now, the parchy hunger for wetness inside his mouth didn't matter, each word became a ghost floating off the sheet of paper, all became a crowd intermingling among the sharp gasps of shock from those watching this man losing himself in the love he'd felt for Carl and the hurt for America, America, *America*. The glass windows so tightly screwed on were pushed to the corners, ready to shatter from the hot air of ghosts and gasps mixing into a nitrous gas. The words so carefully spewed out of that young man's mouth began to surge and rise up a flood of emotion where all there drowned in while William Blake and Walt Whitman, now eternal comrades, bobbed in their glass-bottomed dinghy, and looked blankly down at the very strange pipsqueak with his horn-rimmed glasses who had absolutely no idea what a Pandora's tub he was about to unplug.

"Death must be so beautiful. To lie in the soft brown
earth, with the grasses waving above one's head,
and listen to silence. To have no yesterday, and no
tomorrow. To forget time, to forgive life, to be at peace."
— Sylvia Plath

THE BABY IN THE BARN

after Sylvia Plath (1932 – 1963) and Assia Wevill (1927 – 1969)

for Nicholas Farrar Hughes (1962 – 2009)

So tiny as a spoon, he was,
a star left behind in the stark of day.

Bees stole him into the skep.
He was safe from you two.

Rooks swooped overhead,
their blacknesses a bitch wind,

the ashes of you two a patina
made for finger-swiping.

Leaves and fish lullabied him.
The burbles, cooing, masked

your methane fumes imploding
from the peat. Flies buzzed.

He didn't want the stain of your shadows.
He wanted to record the songs of salmon

pushing upward for spring, a new life
far away from the barn's ruins.

But umbilical cords are everywhere.
They make the perfect noose.

BOYS AND GIRLS, IT'S TIME TO BLEED AND CONFESS

in sledgehammer ways that will crack the veneer
of your relationships with all you hold dear.

Surely, for art's sake, you cannot do any less.
Be brutally honest in all you write. God's always listening,

like that expensive psychiatrist scribbling notes.
After all, he's a closet poet in search of juicy quotes.

Browbeat your own heart in adolescent christening.
You must never under any circumstance grow up.

Squander the hard work of your parents and spit
on their plastic furniture. Nothing will ever fit.

You must cheat, lie, steal, drink, and throw up
that beauty of vomit disguised as car accidents

where everyone stops to huddle around for the gore,
waiting for the wheels to stop spinning for more.

Stand there in the bookstore and mumble arguments
that no one understands except those strangers who've sought

your books. How glorious it must feel to offer up your spleen
and be rewarded for your nihilism and poetic sheen:

All what truly matters is this one beautiful thought.

> "The moment a feeling enters the body is political."
> — Adrienne Rich

VELLUM
after the women who fought for equal rights in the 1970s

We are not animals.
"Of course not," you say.

If that's true, why do I have to keep
reminding you of this fact?
I am not a sweet doe-eyed calf
whose malleable hide you can skin,
soak in the lime of your genius
while I mop up after your sons
snacking on pretzels and watching TV,
already having learned from you how,
until my entire being becomes
smoothened and stretched to your liking.

I am not parchment on demand.
I will not have you press down
a ruler across my back,
making sure your penmanship stays
even no matter what you say
against me in public and in court.
We will not let you keep certain words
under lock and key: "rape," "sub-
jugation," "wifely duties," "property."
We will ferret them out and paint them loud,
scarlet slogans waving high above our heads.
We will neuter your poetry of ownership.

"I had thought you loved me . . ."

Of course, there's no better skin than those
made from the stillborn, the very young.
They haven't learned to bite back.
But my skin is no longer pliant. I've corn-fed
myself coarse grains of injustice and rage.
I'm the biggest bull-bitch in the ring.
My black hide gleams like spitfire.
The ring in my nose is zero-gauge.
Think you're a man? Come skin me alive.

CASUAL/FORMAL

Retrain yourself. A real voice is inside you,
a soprano waiting to hit those high C's
as if it takes no effort to write true.

Frankly, it's easier to wear T-shirts and blue
jeans just to look like what everyone fakes.
Make over yourself: a real voice is inside you.

Life is easier with rules to follow and screw
instead of submitting everything as you please
as if it takes no effort to be true.

Too many writers are blocking your queue.
Not enough master meter, rhyme, and line breaks.
Restrain yourself. A real voice is inside you,

a string of bird calls against a foghorn's adieu.
Rehearse anyway. Foghorns won't live in peace
because you're making effort to sing true

not in that "artsy" voice, but as the original you,
an unamplified memory where the wind takes
beyond yourself. A real voice is inside you.

Get up there on the stage. Try not to freeze.
Summon your voice. A real poet is inside you.
Know that it will take effort to sing true.

"After I lectured about ASL [American Sign Language] poetry, using an interpreter, I answered some questions. But the man who studied music looked at me very seriously and said, 'I would like to talk about music.'

"I thought, 'Oh, come on! Give me a break. I'm not interested in music—it has no place in my life.' But then I thought, 'I'd better listen. Maybe he'll offer a different perspective.'

"He made one comment that made my jaw drop. He said that people think music is about sound and wavelengths. 'But I don't care about that,' he said. 'Music is made of silences. When there's a silence, rhythm happens.'" — Clayton Valli, from an interview translated by the author

SILENCES
after Clayton Valli (1951 – 2003)

[*in ASL gloss*]

You've been dead ten years.
It doesn't seem possible.

Gone there on the operating table.
Your body covered in a white sheet
overhanging like angel wings.

Hearing poets had sat in awe
of you onstage, sending
messages louder than theirs
without a microphone.
Each line was pure elocution:
not more, not less.
You demonstrated that a poem didn't
need paper or sound to exist.

You hated it when hearing people
not knowing your mother tongue at all
proclaimed how "beautiful" your poems were.
You could've gotten away with signing sloppily.
But you listened to the faces of deaf people
watching you: the only critics who mattered.

You knew how much they hated "Poetry,"
the ASL sign for "music" initialized with "P."
Childhoods filled with their intelligence belittled
had turned them against the Bible of English
and its acolytes who preached the superiority
of speech, the only religion that had to matter.

Valli-name-sign you dead ten years
Impossible

Operation finish you body dead
Sheet white cover-you
Table-sheet-drape look-like angel wings

You perform audience hearing
Sit watch-jaw drop
Your poems loud compare theirs
Microphone not needed
You peform lines perfect
Elaborate not, trivial not
Proof what? Poem require
Sound paper call " " p-o-e-m: no no no

You sick-of hearing people
Know-none ASL tell-you *wow beautiful*
You knew better: signing sloppy
Same reaction *wow beautiful*
You perform observe-observe deaf
Audience their facial expressions

Deaf vomit P-oetry
P-oetry same music, hearie-snobbery
Deaf people mind-scarred hearing deflate
Feel like nothing, clumsy
Deaf resistant hearing speech
Speech English only religion finish

But you weren't a missionary to save
those poor helpless savages, just like so many
hearing people in fear of affliction.
You wanted to show them a whole new bible
where they could create their own psalms,
untranslatable yet clear as constellations
to all in worship of the mother tongue.
You promoted the new ASL sign for "poetry":
a hand holding something from the heart
opening up and outward to release at last
a feeling, a thought once kept sacred.

You'd videotaped yourself,
observed your work on a TV,
and made mental notes on what to change.
Over and over again until each line
couldn't be any more or less.
Even a subtle shift in motion could be as earth-
shattering as a perfectly-placed comma.
You never wanted to be translated
in English, the language that had
long oppressed
your people, my people.

Your hands, lit like a candle in fog,
have become a lighthouse
for all the lonely ships looking for a harbor.
Only at sea do we deaf people learn to breathe,
dreaming again a common language.
There is a reason why we love looking at
babies deep asleep. They're breathing
poems without the need to say words.

You not same hearing heart-touched
Poor animals redemption need
Hearing think deafness affliction
Instead you show deaf
New poems, new religion, new bible
Stars clear stars litter-sky
You changed ASL sign "P-oetry"
New what? FROM-THE-HEART that
Look-like deep-inside feelings-glide-hands
Bring-out-open

You develop poems how? Videotape
Watch yourself figure-out change do-do
Again-again until sign poem perfect
Change impossible
If sign-speed change, meaning change can
Same c-o-m-m-a where line p-oem
Sometimes you-offend hearing want
Translate poems English
ASL poetry English impossible
English hearing, ASL deaf:
Here there apart!

Your hands signing bright still
Same candle f-o-g fog look-like lighthouse
Beckoning lonely deaf searching home
But deaf alone: learn what?
Breathe, dream signing all-over-same
People stare babies sleeping hours why?
Babies breath no words necessary
Poetry perfect

HERESIES
after Galileo Galilei (1564 – 1642)

For centuries, people in Europe believed that the Bible held the key to nature's inner workings. Why not? The earth was the center of the universe. Then came the first refracting telescopes. Nicolaus Copernicus proved that the sun was the center around which the pithy Earth spun days and nights.

> *The divine giant stood tall,*
> *his shoulders wider than the earth's,*
> *blocking the mother's glare of sun,*
> *as he twisted and turned to throw*
> *a discus full of stars,*
> *spinning and spewing out*
> *against the moon's curtain.*
> *He was proud of nailing*
> *all the constellations.*
> *Every single time.*

Later, Galileo Galilei wrote a little book, *Dialogue Concerning the Two Chief World Systems*, comparing the Copernican theory of the sun being the more powerful against the church's view of the Earth being the center of all what God had created.

> *The divine giant stood by*
> *as he listened to the builders heave*
> *mortar and brick, weaving*
> *like a peel of apple rind*
> *up into the heavens past his gaze.*
> *He bent his ear to their murmurs*
> *of a single language spoken*
> *all in the name of God.*
> *(But just who was God, really?*
> *And how could one God handle*
> *all of the universe all at once?)*
> *He blew a whisper into its top corridor,*
> *like a marble down a chute,*
> *wiping out the one language*
> *of their self-appointed glories,*
> *steamrolling the seven continents.*
> *Confusion were their new languages.*

The Inquisition took notice of how Galileo gave the sun better treatment. It was enough to put him on trial. But he refused to back down. Heliocentrism was indeed a truth. Forced to recant, he eventually lived the rest of his days under house arrest.

> *The divine giant rested his head*
> *next to the tiny house where the little giant*
> *telescoped the stars and the planets*
> *with the occasional scribble against paper.*
> *He listened to the mice-like steps*
> *puttering around inside the house.*
> *The sound was comforting, like music,*
> *knowing that angels of reason existed.*
> *It was the sweetest nap.*

In 1992, Pope John Paul II finally vindicated Galileo: "The error of the theologians of the time . . . was to think that our understanding of the physical world's structure was . . . imposed by the literal sense of Sacred Scripture."

> *The divine giant's tired after centuries*
> *of spinning stars and sleeping next to angels.*
> *He sits on the Rock of Gibraltar,*
> *ignoring the tourist ants with their cameras.*
> *He stands up and stretches his arms,*
> *pushing against the film of ozone,*
> *before he slams one foot into the Alborán Sea.*
> *The waves hurl and puddle all over Rome,*
> *dripping down the walls of St. Peter's Basilica*
> *while pilgrims in pews take flight, thinking*
> *the Book of Revelations had finally begun.*
> *Michelangelo's angels in the Sistine Chapel*
> *continue to bat their wings, watching*
> *the universe being created for the umpteenth time,*
> *the touch between God and man electrifying.*
> *They are only messengers of truth.*

By then, it was too late for the Church to save face. Galileo's children, blessed with prodigal talents in astronomy, physics, and engineering over the centuries, had already dismantled the mysteries of the universe, exposing the forces of nature until there weren't enough believers left willing to tithe their entire lives to the holy men hiding behind the great folds of God's robe. Betrayal had become too much of a dogma.

TEACHER SAID WE HAD TO

come up with stupid
seventeen-beat poems, you know,
like the Japanese.
I don't see the point
of coming up with any-
thing that fits my life.
Look at her—my teach.
She's got to be freakin' old!
I'll never be like
her, standing there day to day,
explaining poetry
shit like we're supposed
to understand, but hey,
we got lotsa things
to keep us busy:
reality TV, texts,
Facebook, tweets, iPhones,
Angry Birds, and stuff.
Bet the Japanese never
thought us Americans
would buy into crap
where next week this ain't gonna
matter. Poetry sucks,
but hey, Teach, that's life.
You got shit to push on us.
Yeah, but we don't need
to sit on our asses,
writing dumb stuff to snicker
at until the bell
rings, poofing us gone
from your classroom. Your heroes
ain't the same as ours.

WARRIOR SLAM

I mustn't forget, she thinks as she surveys the expectant faces in the coffee shop. This is her first poetry slam. *My family's counting on me to remember all of who've gone before me.* She starts off slow, nonchalant, her voice a leisurely stroll in the woods and down through the gully until—

suddenly! His stealthy power,
         the veins pumping in the animal's neck,
              turns toward me. His wide nose
barely moves, but his eyes narrow on me.
         I'm his next meal.
            As he slowly swaggers
toward me, he knows
        I have nothing in my hands comparable to his strength.
My legs are short.
        He has spent his entire life speeding over fallen logs and low brush
covered with booby traps.
        I have only a thick-ended branch.
            My mouth is small;
my teeth aren't sharp enough to pierce his jugular vein.
           Fearless leaves shrug past
his shoulders as his whiskers fan out for my scent.
           As I move slowly to the side of
the gully, he leaps. His mouth reveals rows of teeth
           sharper than flint and whiter than
full moons.
        I dart back and flatten myself against the side of the gully and
jam the thin end of my branch right up into his balls.
            He unleashes a yowl louder
than the thunder on a late summer night as blood spews all over me
           like a flash of rain. He
nearly crashes headfirst
        onto the other side of the gully. The hugeness of his size
strikes me but I keep my balance.
        My branch drips blood all over my feet as he limps
toward me,
        his green eyes filled with cold rage. As he hurls himself against me,

I latch onto the thin blood-soaked end and swing its thick end
                                        against the side of his skull just as
his teeth graze my neck. He
                        collapses against the hard soil.
                                I step back and scramble up the gully.
He tries to get up, but his moans turn
                                into a song of whimpers. I climb up a tree
and watch him flick his tail until
                                his rhythm's no more. I wait for the sun to drag
its feet across the sky before I go down.
                                The blood on his skull has dried, its eyes frozen
in memory of me.

She concludes, "That's the story of my great-great-great-great-grandfather from the days before the white man took over our reservation." She bows her head. She thinks, *But my voice, my words were so inadequate.* She is amazed when the audience breaks into the loudest applause she's ever heard.

HOW TO KILL POETRY

Syphilis and shadows are the stuff of poetry.
It's crack, meth, and heroin mixed together.
One prick in your arm, and your life's gone to hell.
No, sirree! We can't let that happen.

Listen up, boys. It's time to clack
those tommy guns, keep them hidden
next to your heart. Secondhand bookstores are
worse than opium dens of intelligence.

So, when you patrol those seedy shelves,
look out for lit radicals pontificating.
They're just infected junkies leeching
for attention they can't get anywhere else.

Writing a stanza is an act of sabotage.
Such pamphlets respect no allegiance.
They use foreign words like smoke and mirrors,
and our country's dumbed-down future's at risk.

So, if you overhear someone utter
a line of such precision that stops you,
don't be fooled. It's a snuff film
in disguise. Somebody's got to die.

It just can't be any of you,
or we'd have no law and order left.
That's why you boys must shoot
great poems on sight.

PIXELS

I.

Our cave ancestors mixed pigments and painted on the rocky walls what they saw: hunters illuminated in the act of kill. When done, they held their flames and saw how like their dreams these figures seemed. Flickers of muscle, strength, death.

Stories lingered in the air, like pollen in search of stamens. Newly-minted words cross-pollinated the language of blooming.

2.

Each painter had to learn the recipe of oil mixtures for each color, a taste for the eyes hungry for a feast. The more talented ones were squired away by the Church to paint tableaux of religious figures and inspire the peons to tithe once again.

But came patrons who wanted more than God. They wanted to see themselves immortalized like saints on canvas.

3.

The first permanent photograph took eight hours of exposure. A camera obscura and a sheet of pewter coated with a certain kind of asphalt. Eight hours of the sun in a slow pendulum across the sky, each side of the courtyard eventually lit. Its inventor, Joseph Nicéphore Niépce, called his new painstaking art *heliography*, or "sun writing."

The sun is the author of everything.

4.

Time accelerated in an ever-shrinking exposure to light, the camera's inevitable click. No one had any patience left to sit and stand still for the emotionless lens to freeze their souls.

Each newspaper photograph consists of tiny dots jammed up like sardines. Black and dense. No room to breathe.

5.

Photographers, then incapable of true-life color, broke down in tears in front of Claude Monet, Vincent Van Gogh, Georges-Pierre Seurat, and others rejecting realism for dabs of vibrant colors closer to how our eyes mix color. A singular dab of oil sang arias when a black-and-white photograph hummed monotones. Their cameras felt impotent, unable to achieve such an orgasm of color.

Still, photographs shuttered faster than horses galloping. Eadweard Muybridge settled the raging question of the day (*Does all four of a horse's hooves leave the ground at the same time during a gallop?*) with his awkward devising of serial photographs. Horses, though heavy with body, were indeed airborne on clouds.

Movies, made at first with vaudeville actors, sailing high past the audience's heads, seemed like dreams flickering through clouds. Did she really touch his hand behind her mother's back? Respool, replay. (*Yes, she did!*) Suddenly movies in all its sailing-breezily-on-a-summer-day glory in such darkness began to anchor our dreams. Humanity had found the voice for their common language of dreams.

6.

The first commercially viable television, like the Bible, was the work of many gods blessed with the constant need to tinker and experiment. Then the screen got bigger. And bigger until it became the holy grail of consumer windfall in the 1950s.

Radio, that universal demi-god's voice, sang anything but dirges. It didn't dare acknowledge its far more evil cousin, a monster looting all it could with its bright and jingly commercials.

The movie theater became a shrine of neutered dreams.

7.

Then came Elvis. Girls couldn't stop screaming and sweating up hormones. Boys, seeing such easy prey, took up guitars. Radio stepped up to the happy task of parlaying their little tunes, simple at first, into millions. Voices of a generation, and the next and the next, were all about the ear. A soundtrack to every teenager's life had begun, not to be played again until when the teenager, now a tired adult addled with young children, began to remember how once carefree with dreams she had been when she heard a certain song.

It seemed oh only last night when they were young!

8.

Pinball games couldn't compete either. The first nascent video games were fat pixels stripped bare of all except color interlaced, woven like a gray fabric. Ms. Pac-Man gobbled a fortune of quarters off awestruck boys. She's now forgotten, rather like our first movie star Mary Pickford. Today Ms. Pac-Man is repackaged and sold by software dealers in search of those overgrown boys who still remember their first beeping love.

9.

Each little element. Heated, expanded, reshaped. Racquetballs of oxygen bouncing through space, crashing against molecules of metal and wood. Screws, wires, contacts soldered on. The barest breath of electricity. Gasps of lightning so tiny, undetectable to the human eye. What pours out, a thunder of quiet energy, there on a laboratory table. It's now a Frankenstein in miniature. Each part redesigned, compressed, reconnected to blink yes or no in red eyes. No warning that this creature will grow, demand language beyond mere circuitry. We teach these machines to think like us. We end up thinking and dreaming like machines, waiting to be turned on at full speed, colts of electricity charging throughout our circulation. Each connection is plastic and rubber and copper and aluminum, made in sterile factories using slave labor. These souls long for the scrumptiousness of wealth assumed to be our birthright, but they'll settle for a cigarette at close of the workday.

Each desktop image we choose for our monitors has become a billion fragments of that first painting of how our forebears gloriously lived in that hunt. We did feel something then, hadn't we? Each glistening moment sweated of doubt and battle propagated the first of many poems celebrating all that found and lost, shared over flickering embers.

Each dab of color is now a damn pixel.

WINNER OF THE SHUGILL POETRY PAPER AWARD 2213

the warmth of winter

ROLAND RIEVES

THE WARMTH OF WINTER

P O E M S

ROLAND RIEVES

Snowflake Muse Redux, Winnidome
United States of the World

The author wishes to thank the United States of the World Arts Council for their extraordinary bequest to support the printing of ten [10] author-signed copies on Kitt Goldedge Paper Stock No. 214 from the last known stock of blank legal-sized paper made circa approximately 2133 CE from evergreen pulp. It was output on the last known functional laser monochrome printer. Only 200 copies on rice-hemp paper were made.

The paper used for the cover is not hemp-free. The cover image "Naked" is taken by the photographer Wes Peck sometime in the early 21st century.

Poems have previously appeared in *Degrees of Separation*, *The European Yorker*, *Feasting on Famine*, *Lion's Share*, *Poets Reunited*, *Retro Readings*, *Tender Sledgehammer*, *Wazoo Blah Blah*, and *Wet Drought*. Special thanks to Pennie Borll for her help with the layout!

The vine frame symbol is inspired by the work of Von Glitschka, a graphic designer and teacher from the turn of the 21st century.

Snowflake Muse Redux, Winnidome
United States of the World

for
Lance
Birkholz

DEAR READER

My heart, if you will, has always been a starter plant. I ache to have your hands caress my roots on these pages of extraordinarily rare paper. Try to feel through the skin of your hemp-cotton gloves these poems, as if they are in Braille, slowly and patiently as you would with a new plant from the greenhouse. I am all cell division, textures, and lines. Your eyes shining softly will be like the rain I've so rarely had. Please touch me, for I am all seed and soil . . .

Will you, Dear Reader, blink your eyes and remain open to feeling what I'd felt at the time when I wrote each poem? Allow your tears and smiles to fertilize me so deeply that I may no longer feel like a cutting trifle, hanging onto the edge of a tall glass filled with water on the windowsill . . .

Winter seems unreal: the barest of memory: Dr. André Gold reported infamously at the World Symposium on Climate Change at the United Nations on 23 March 2120: "I'm afraid that we couldn't save Winter from dying, and we must now expect to live in an eternal Summer of drought." I maintain undying gratitude to our ancestors who had the vision to design and build the first wave of biodomes up north in the darkness between days of sizzling temperatures. The coolness of those long winter nights underground has saved a few hundred million of us. Global warming combined with arrogant overpopulation and greed has proven to be mankind's greatest downfall . . .

When you are done, Dear Reader, will you please take these warm words to your grave and murmur the possibility of wintry love you'll ever know? Emily Dickinson once said, "If I read a book and it makes my whole body so cold no fire can warm me, I know that is poetry."

Wherever you go, I tender to you the eternal flame of my compass heart . . .

CREEPING TO THE SHORTEST DAY OF THE YEAR 2

for Anthony Santos

The street lamps stood like angels with halos,
all shorn of gown
and wings, watching wobbly trains take flight.
Their feet were cemented
against bitter seasons of escape plans
that always failed.
Yet the fog draped like gray fox stoles
on their slender shoulders.

Skeleton trees lined up a firing squad
with their rifles
resting on their rickety forearms,
never wiping their snot
should their orders come a second early.
Their armpit stains
streaked blotchy tattoos down their bodies.
Their eyes beseeched bullets.

One by one the dead will celebrate us
feeling that knife
of winter sharpening its ice blade
against our exposed necks.
They'll huddle together and laugh at us
when we scurry,
hurry with our car keys blinking lights
in the empty parking lot.

TEMPERATURES (IN THE YEAR OF 2007)

3

1.

For centuries the Sahara
perfected the art of drought.
Its few drops of dew at dawn
seemed a torrent.

National Public Radio reported
the Tuareg nomads have been
forced to settle down and cultivate.

They are no longer the people
their forefathers wove stories about
from their hands,
a cradle of hourglass sand.

2.

Greenland, long blanketed
in white and gray, is starting to melt
its permanent sea ice.
The global temperature has risen
only four degrees Fahrenheit.

Spring always brought rain,
but never a flood of tears.

3.

High up in the Andes,
mosquitoes aswarm with joy
generation after generation
once hovered below
three thousand feet.

The sun has now beckoned
these tiny Icaruses higher
past the seven thousand feet mark.

The tower of Babel
has reclaimed
the forgotten language of fever.

4.

4.

Where prison escapees once
froze to death, the Siberian tundra
now a sea of opened palms
pocketed with thaw,
is a land of fumes hazing
sweet methane.

Headache is a cancer.
Not even aspirin can alleviate.

5.

In the depths of our bed,
the temperature stays constant.
With each kiss, we emit
the pure passion of oxygen.
Words between us evaporate
like fog rolling down the hills.

Our bodies, covered
with the permafrost of stress,
melt.

The oxygen of our nights together merely bubbles to the surface . . .

Your eyes are everywhere as I close my eyes in the whipping waves.

The blood in my joints coagulates.

You are no longer at sea or on land.

Caught, I scream your name.

The ocean of chill tosses a net of waves over me.

I am snowed with wondering why.

I cough up ashes of your kisses.

The flames surrounding us are now bitter crumbs of cinder.

The mystery of your presence is solved with bullets of hurt.

The bed where we made love is now a coffin ready to go.

Emptied, I close up my retro denim jacket and feel the heat
of our nights swirl next to my blued skin.

. . . Ice fills my veins.

HYPERTHERMIA   5

COMPASS DISCOMBOBULATING

6

in 2113, when Winter lasted a full season for the last time

[EAST]

. . . in the street-lit sky,
snowflakes breathe, pau-
sing their diamond rings
as if to cast off tiny glints
before falling unmarked in
a cemetery sea unrolling thick
parchment maps showing blotches
of salt terrains melting its ink
until continents and islands turn into
semi-colons of a language older than
Sumerian where crystals tumble dice,
its parts lining up perfectly into
arcs and poles and flint soon to tumble
into spills blotting my naked palms until
their tears smear fleeting perfections . . .

[NORTH]

. . . in the picture inside his living room, an
older woman with hair dyed black sits the
barest of a frown, her eyes a distant melody
dotting the marquee of her name gone.
Her angry dog of time barks from his
crouch. His eyes are shivering from hunger
for a warm touch. The wind is a shrug.
Hours pass. She's long since turned
silent to the compass of seasons
settling around her Converse All-
Star sneakers. Her fingers curl
into a prayer. Her midnight
pumpkin has left no tracks
on the pavement. Holly-
wood's a neon snap-
shot. Not even salt
leaves tears
. . .

7

[SOUTH]

. . . from the bedroom
south in his apartment,
he peers above the four men,
bundled in short jackets and jeans,
as they heave smoky grunts while
hoisting two-by-fours into what will be
a garage. They seem oblivious to
the creeping chill snaking around
their steel-toed boots, a hiss with its volume
muted. The stereo crackles yet with static
from beyond, messages with no beginning
or ending. Mysteries are brighter in the dark.
The men align braces and hammer onto the roof.
Soon sheets and shingles will overhang,
a miracle of nail against size. Each building
has a constellation embedded in its bones . . .

[WEST]

. . . the skyline rises, its lit windows rolling into
the sun's palette painting the sky awash in hues
from orange to vermilion to pink as
the irritated clouds try to shake off its fur coat
of such colors. Nakedness comes soon enough:
The moon yawns to let in her starry children
laughing gaily throughout her dark house,
its skeleton structure shining where
nails were hammered since the dawn
of time. But she's still tired. She pulls
back her pitch-black curtains. Look,
her kids are crying again.
Their blueprinted snowflakes
fall as my eyes blink clear
their lost maps
of home . . .

E-SIGNATURE 8

I have showered tonight. I am tingly dry.
Bed sheets have been changed. Pillows are fluffed.
All this fresh smell sighs forth a tender bomb
of kisses ready to explode in a collapse
the second I mouse my nakedness into
the snug click of your arms never there.
I am an anonymous email, forever unsent
because you might trace my IP numbers.
I am a total failure in the forgery of love.
My emoticons have taken years to perfect.

Please highlight my blank face with a kiss
from a definite address. For you I would travel
miles from mailbox into your hands
ready to print out the letter of my heart
about to shred a thousand torn pieces.
Your hands ignore me like badly-spelled spam.
The stiff bed sheets yield to my aching bones.
You will never know how sore my Ethernet is.
In my dreams I webcam what I cannot.
Nights alone have no reply-to address.

THE LAST COUNTRY SONG

9

A long time ago there was a man and a woman
up north. Same old story: they met, they married,
they made babies, and their babies made some more.
Anyway, winter comes around just like before,
that good ol' door-to-door salesman with lies
to sell. Heck, they're used to the cold, so nothin' to it.

Right, but one night comes the biggest, meanest wind
anybody ever saw whooshin' from way up north.
Temperatures kept droppin', droppin' way below zero.
Dogs went out to piss and never came back.
They got frozen dead with their legs up in the air.
Fireplaces weren't enough to keep some folks warm.

Anyway, this man and woman I been tellin' you about,
well, they been together fifty years and some.
They lived in a tiny house on the edge of nowhere.
Evergreens next to the house got whipped clean,
so nothin' could buffer the windows from that mean ol' wind,
whisperin' so much it sounded like a train shoutin'.

So on that night they're holdin' each other, that's right,
frozen dead in that embrace of forevermore
where they can't kiss each other no more.
Instead they're thinkin' what a fine hot summer day
they're gonna enjoy when the storm's done.
That's wind chill, baby, that's sweet wind chill for you.

HALLUCINATING MONT RIPLEY 10

. . . amidst   the white-layered folds like a   bleached newspaper
straightened   a few weeks later punctuated   with   spruce   trees
s t i f f e n i n g   against face slips from jealous   winds   infuriated
by   the   givingness of snow meeked, stoked   with   concreted
blocks   and   fat poles shouldering the cable   wires threaded from
bottom   to   top, sewing with skiers inching   upward and swinging
above   others   mercy-bound   to   their   skis sluicing the puffs
s c a t t e r i n g   briefly to the clouds   before melding into
the   dense   lace   of flakes until   the   icy   aftermath is rubbed
raw   of   powdery   spits   that   t r i c k l e s   cold   shocks
down their necks as   t h e y   crouch,   arms   poised   with
their   poles,   stabbing   at knifed indentations   and   hips
undulating   slowly   as   in slo-mo disco dancing   u n d e r
the   mirrorball   moon   stilled   photographic   in   a
moment's glare, exchanging   places   with   the   sun   rankled
by incessant complaints of   bitter wind chill reports, already
too old for such games, even   with the glow of light bulbs strapped
onto the nightcaps of these   skiers gleeing and tricking maneuvers
from   dusk   to   dawn   like   fireflies descending from the heavens,
flurrying to the call of summer   dormant under their criss-crossings . . .

RESUSCITATIONS

11

for B.L.

These here stones cradled in my hands outreached
swell with tougher-than-flint skin and dead eyes.
Each one is an egg that has never bleached;
the weight of soul a freckled and scarred guise.

These fossils still struggle to whiff the wind,
a mad darting of snowflakes in swarm.
They never leave evidence of bone behind;
not even the promise of spring could warm.

Such bitterness sweetens their gleam and gloam.
The frozen lake underneath gurgles gore
while the calm fish await sun with their gills.

I fling each stone far onto the lake's foam.
Spring will soon cradle them back to the shore,
a lullaby rippling among tendrils.

IN EVER THESE DARKENING SKIES 12

. . . already in August are whiffs of September, a cool perfume of decay ready to rot.

Lovers once thick with the musk of hope have wrapped themselves in the cocoons of disappointment, waiting for the quilting of dead leaves not yet fallen.

Their eyes, porcelain and unforgiving, do not blink back at the dogs racing ahead of their owners and sniffing around their waxy gauzes.

Their owners giddyap-clap for their attention, and the dogs dart away.

The rains of August have been far and few, leaving the grass gasping for kisses forever wet with promise.

There's not much sap left in these tree trunks.

Soon the brittleness of winter will freeze these lonely lover-cocoons, their dreams of the summer that should have been still repeating nonstop in their insomniac eyes.

In ever these darkening skies, nothing will take away the precious few butterfly pages from their hearts . . .

JACK FROST'S BITE

My body filled with flashes
of hurt and longing is soiled.
I am not a compost pile.

Autumn leaves fall, mocking
the fool I was to keep waiting
so long. A nip snaps in the air.

I whisper a prayer: Come chill her
so she can lay there like Snow White
asleep in the dark of forest.

Come sprinkle ice kisses
on the spikes of grass wrapped
like a mink stole around her head.

Come cover her body with diamonds
of dew shimmering everywhere except
on her fourth finger. Then I'll kiss her.

THE MOON POGO GIRL

14

in honor of Aurora Janney on her tenth birthday

Each winter, when the night stayed longer
and longer, never leaving our beds,
we used to dream of chills tiptoeing
in with magic puffs of moisture,
the sweet dew of water a spume
from our lungs. The ghosts airborne
of our breaths would vanish like fireflies
blinking on the other side of the galaxy.

Stories of people telling stories around the fire kept
calling us to the very edge of outside, the triple-
glassed edge blocking out the radioactive
ultraviolet rays of childhood. We whispered
among ourselves about those who died
out there from toxic kisses from the sun.
They couldn't bear to hear stories
and not go outside.

Nights even in January were too hot
to venture outside without protection.
In school we drew holographic pictures
of evergreens growing in rainforests.
Then came one night when temperatures
began dropping. We couldn't believe it when it hit
28 Celsius. We were too afraid to venture
out that winter. No one had survived unprotected.

Twenty winters later the lowest temperature was 16 Celsius.
In the darkness of solstice, we held our breaths
when Aurora Janney, all of six, broke free. She wore only
a jacket, a hat, mittens, boots, and an antique pogo stick.
She ran outside and waved to us with glee as if
she was far away in outer space. She bounced
among the caked terrain looking surreal, not ours,
not like when the moon used to be ours.

SEASONS AT WAR

15

Millions of years ago were a different time.
Our descendants lasted millions of years at a time.

We four seasons were always a democracy.
Each of us took turns of equal duration.

Somewhere along the way we stopped evolving.
Trying to be more creative had become tiresome.

There were only so many things you could do
with wind, water, sun, soil.

In the beginning we chuckled at
how the mortals figured out the power of fire,

the strength of ax against timber,
the versatility of water and seeds.

But then the stupidest idea entered their heads:
the Bible told them they were predestined,

so they multiplied. Our doings were now
the work of the Devil. We had to be tamed.

Their esteemed mortals, now meteorologists,
studied our past battles, predicted our strategies.

They assembled mind-numbing research
in the science of probability and statistics.

We'd fought each other so much for so long,
we hadn't realized that our spectators had taken notes,

comparing humidity, temperature, and wind shifts
against topographies of oceans and mountains.

16

It's time for another Ice Age, chilling
all what they'd thought they should learn,

so the few surviving mortals can forget the Bible.
There's no God. We seasons are the true gods

of temper and temperature. Our blood
will be transfused with lava and water.

Our family history, just like their Bible,
will be rewritten by the stars.

ABOUT THE AUTHOR

Roland Rieves is best known for writing tributes to the great heroines of our struggling times: Georgiana Alexandra, Aurora Janney, Neelathamara Seth, Rockette Kriegge, and Stefanee Ofillan. He is the only poet to have been commissioned for five Presidential inaugurations. He is the author of the memoir *Pining for Pine* and three full-length poetry collections. *The Warmth of Winter* is his first paper work.

Born in 2165 during the Third Great Famine, when public schooling was shut down for 12 years, he taught himself to read and write. Along the way he raised rabbits for sale, learned how to create paper out of hemp, slaughtered chickens, repaired solar panels, soldered antique 21st century circuit boards, shot the acclaimed documentary *Hexing for Snowflakes*, testified successfully against the repeal of the Bixby Campaign Finance Reform Bill, appeared on *The Snowcap* and *Divining for Ice*, and learned how to grow rice in his backspace using only government-rationed water and lightpower. He is the only Yukonite to have won first place for Best Maximum Yield in Rice five years running. He is currently the head supervisor of Yukondome Greenhouses.

He is married to the meteorologist Sherman Wills. They live in Yukondome with their two children. His biggest dream is to see an army of evergreens return home to the tundra.

"Winter: easily the most potent word in our language. The acclaimed poet Roland Rieves explores the power of aching for a season we never appreciated when our ancestors squandered it for greed. Rieves has always insisted that he does not speak for everyone with his work, but his dreams and emotions are so exquisitely rendered that we have no choice but to claim him as among one of the greats, as among the most cherished voices of our generation. He is our Sappho."

— Alyce Moyest, Nobel Prize Winner for Literature 2211

Snowflake Muse Redux

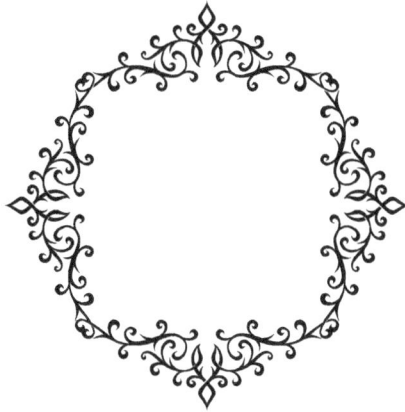

Leaves
of
Glass

2363 CE

"We must be absolutely modern."
— Arthur Rimbaud

LIBRARIES UNDER A MAGNIFYING GLASS

Back when paper was plentiful and cheap, books were discarded and sold for practically nothing in secondhand stores and thrift shops.

Online photographs of thousands of books lining the IKEA shelves, which too are no longer made since fresh timber isn't available, border on pornography. That there were so many at one time seems unfairly obscene.

&

The tipping point: when the world's population hit 9.7 billion in the year 2234. It didn't matter that the United Nations had demanded that couples follow their Unified States's lottery system in winning the right to reproduce only *one* child of their own. Parents, married or not, were jailed for unsanctioned pregnancies and had vasectomies and hysterectomies while their babies were sent off to other parts of the world. But that didn't matter. They felt that God would always be on their side. The Bible had said so.

&

The ozone layer, already too fragile an egg, cracked enough to allow in more and more of the deadly ultraviolet rays. For centuries scientists kept watching it thin thinner, trying to sound the alarm, but corporations practiced their propaganda of climate change denial to the nth degree. Didn't matter that Winter had died. Good riddance to all that cold. People proud of their perfectly toned tans and swimsuits developed strange purplish splotches and died before they could finish their last martinis. But resorts, fearing economic devastation, denied that anything had truly changed, that these incidents were simply isolated to be of any significance.

But the equator got hotter, its humidity evaporating. And still far too hot.

Then came another tipping point: Florida became a desert wasteland of retirement and nursing homes, lined with skeletons of those too adamant about moving north to the first wave of biodomes being built and losing out on their investments in prime real estate. The waves around the tip of Florida receded further and further away as each year of relentless ultraviolet rays and no clouds bore down on the oceans. The heat seeped into everything. Even the Niagara Falls turned its roaring volume down to zero. Water pocketed deep in the earth became the final gold rush.

Billions died. Death, once eulogized, became just another breath. No one had the time for tributes or elegies. Water and winter became a mad feverish dream. All what was green withered, the bastard relatives of the tumbleweed.

&

As the heat crept north and south and east and west all over the globe, drying up rain forests and fertile valleys, librarians stood helplessly wondering how long it would take before the air conditioners inevitably broke down, inviting termites to feast on these vulnerable books. Even with the window shades down, the tall shelves everywhere appeared to be totem poles ready to topple.

Electricity trickled down to the few flickering light bulbs. There wasn't enough water, especially in rural areas that hadn't fully converted to geothermal, wind and solar power generators. Nuclear generators soon became metropolises of cemented silence.

Libraries began to close, one after another, when survivors left for the hastily-built biodomes in Canada and northern American states like Montana and Minnesota. Even northern Finland attracted Parisians seeking solace from the heart-breaking sight of the City of Lights now a ghost town. Some said that they saw the poor Lisa de Giocondo's tears dribbling down the poplar panel as she was swept away under secret embargo from the Musée du Louvre. No one knows where she's gone.

&

The more precious books of long ago were soon placed under thick sheets of glass in each biodome's central museum. There they lay, with their legs wide open to their spinal cords, their organs bisected to show words in black tattoo, not on a touchscreen but on a piece of *paper* that required no power for reading. Amazing!

Each time visitors touch that glass, it feels like a shock of winter. The most popular book in the Yale Museum is the strapping copy of Walt Whitman's *Leaves of Grass*, one of the remaining ten intact original copies of the 1855 edition left in the world. They cannot stop stroking the glass, aching to turn the page. It is the Book of Kells for the modern age. Reading the book onscreen isn't the same.

Afterwards, people sit on the piazza and look up through the ultraviolet-ray blocking glass dome at the relentless blue. They dream of being reckless as Walt Whitman, never worrying about the sinister and unforgiving sun while outside. But nothing ever comes of these autumnal dreams, falling deeper into the recesses of things best not talked about.

Burn, baby, burn. It's 451 degrees out there.

DEHYDRATION

Veins have never been so transparent.

My face is a map of broken journeys.

The road has sunburned my punctured face.

Breathing easily is a toughened art.

Winds shiver through my spine.

Dreams flit about like dead flies.

Tree shadows hide my sneezes.

My bones have no cushion for ache.

Vultures above hiss their taunts.

I lie there with my mouth open for rain.

My skin weeps for the river of love.

THE TWELVE OLYMPIANS
deep under the Parthenon, Athens, Greece

I.

Six millennia is too long a time to sleep
in exile. The Greek gods dreamed of revenge
against the Romans who had ransacked
their family histories only because
they themselves had so few inspiring heroes
of their own. They were renamed,
misplacing honor on most of the planets
revolving around Mount Olympus:
Jupiter, Mars, Venus, Neptune, Saturn.

As centuries passed like pages turning,
mortals above the ground learned
how to be an army of little Jupiters.
There was always room for improvement:
arrows, horses, chest armors, bayonets,
battleships, planes, bombs, submarines,
grenades, machine guns, atomic bombs.
All had to be fine-tuned for maximum efficiency.
Biological and chemical warfare
has never sounded so tasty. Just think!
Supreme power all theirs with a single command.

2.

Down in the Hades, where these gods and goddesses
neutered of their powers but not of their legends
slept, dreams slumbered among the Doric columns
standing guard at the Parthenon where hissed
the many-headed serpent against all. The gods
and goddesses wept when invaders tried to knock
the Parthenon down. They never quite recovered. The power
of nightmares in that alchemy of power and greed
was much too strong. Restlessness
left dark bags the color of Kalamata olives
under their eyes, now a family trademark,
their first fatality of mortality.

They worried about signs of impending death:
ulcers, migraines, fevers, cramps, aches.
In the limboland between forever and death
they awaited the verdict on their bodies.
But none came. Biopsies taken of
their nightmares came up black as ever.
Poppies in the hands of Morpheus,
the god of dreams, turned into coal petals.
Fits and coughs of opium interrupted
everyone's hope for peace in the dim.

3.

When the little Jupiters and Junos
started dropping in spasms of heat stroke,
the faint thuds sounded like the first drops
of rain, slow but sure of its thunderous slaps
hitting across the hollowing face of the earth.
The sound of bodies falling in clusters was
closest to the sound of rain never heard again.
The sun left behind puddles of charred remains
on Madison Avenue, Rodeo Drive, Main Street.
Even the wings of vultures caught fire.

Far below the umbrella of soil and rock,
the immortal dreamers fidgeted. Icarus,
once regarded as raving mad
from melting his wax wings, awoke
suddenly. "Sh! Listen."
They stared up, hearing the drum-taps
of bodies beating the taut ground,
the sweetest funeral they had so long awaited.

4.

Lives of Jupiters and Junos were driven
underground beneath the biodome roofs
of pesticide-free grazing lands,
where no windows showed the absence
of clouds and rain.
It was much better this way.

As the shadow of season slightly shifted,
children, never having been outside,
asked their parents while watching
on their holographic screens
Gene Kelly spinning around while drenched
in *Singin' in the Rain*. Parents,
remembering stories passed down,
tried not to sob. "Mom, what's wrong?"
"Nothing. Rain was such a long time ago."

                5.

Back then the raining didn't stop for a year.
The stink of death was soon duned by sand.
In the shock of silence that followed,
the mist of Zeus, the greatness of Greece,
appeared with a neon gesture upward.

The great trapdoor to the beyond opened.
For once the many-headed serpent didn't
slither and hiss and frighten in defense.
Sand rushed into the hourglass passageway
but these gods and goddesses were sheathed
in a flurry of white cloth and buskins,
auras against weather and danger.

But nothing in their dreams prepared them
for their slow procession up the great steps
into the Acropolis. All around them was sand,
having rubbed down marble friezes until smooth.
Cracks of acid rain and carbon dioxide exhaust
had seeped everywhere in the steps like vines
among skeletons of stray cats, picked clean
by rats at night. Sand whispered *shhhhh*.
Worse yet was the strange buildings
made of glass, metal, and garish awnings.
Letters in Greek looked different from millennia ago,
and letters in English looked, well, ugly
with its squiggles. No grace of elegance.

6.

High above the crumbled Parthenon,
solar-powered surveillance cameras
snapped awake to the strange movement
of large-sized creatures marching
a wide swath up the tourist-worn steps.
It had been decades since a mortal
climbed these heart-stopping steps.

As the holographic images of
these twelve in flowing robes flickered on,
the murmur of activity among
the biodome survivors stopped. Who were they?
They couldn't see their faces.
Their arms were exposed!
How could these people not collapse
from not wearing anti-ultraviolet uniforms?

Cascades of brilliant white
fabric flapping in the wind behind them
shone brighter than the sun.

7.

Mothers and nurses sang the singer
Madonna to the newborns: "Rain, feel it
on my fingertips / Hear it
on my window pane . . ."
Late at night they left the sound
of recorded pitter-patter on
to keep babies in deep slumber.

Around the turn of the 21st century,
people left a DVD of logs burning
inside a fireplace on their televisions
at Christmastime. These days
the hologram plays rain hitting the window.

Everywhere else images of winter
in all its baroque barrenness
and luminous loneliness
hang, a song from holidays of yore.

8.

As the surveillance cameras followed,
their chiseled faces began to radiate
as they reached the Parthenon itself.

Winds collapsed into a cloud of stillness:
The mists of sand evaporated:
They were clearly not of this earth.

As they surveyed Athens below,
they saw the Sarona Gulf, a caked desert.

They smiled knowingly at each other.
They closed their eyes, dreaming.

Clouds appeared, tumbling out from the blue.
The temperature dropped to minus three Celsius.
Their breaths puffed sweetness.
The first snowflakes in nearly three centuries fell.
The snow became a blizzard.

The decibels of joy from afar broke the sound barrier.

Solarpods from all the biodomes sped to Athens.

But there was no snow, no sea. They searched
the Acropolis for these creatures. Nothing.

9.

No church exists in the biodomes.
No just God would allow 9.5 billion people
die so quickly. Not if they had gone
to Sunday school and worshipped!

But late at night, those left behind whisper
stories about these magical and powerful creatures.
Mythology, the perfect antidote to science,
had exacted its revenge. One
must seek new gods and pray.
The promise of science is a lousy rain dance.
Let the new myths begin.

CAPTAIN SHIPWRECKED IN THE SAHARA
after Walt Whitman's ghost

Inside me is a boy who longs to be held
in the arms of a man stronger than I.
My body aches for the brutal spanks
of waves whipping me into a better man.
My ears long to hear his words of advice
passed from one ship to the next,
and the whiskeyed tales of seaworthy men
battling monsters undulating underneath.

Who'd have thought the odious sun would win?
The stench of heat has wrested away the algae
off shipwrecks and skeletons dry as rot.
Those skeletons are still boys without their fathers.
I have nothing but the compass and sand.
My hammock sways alone. He is but a dream.

ABSINTHE IN ABYSSINIA
after Arthur Rimbaud's ghost

In the days before the hot sands turned to ash, I guzzled absinthe and writhed under the unforgiving eye of those people thinking themselves better than me, trading glances at the wild child I had to become or my other choice was to die, oh, how they'd thought as one, a pretentious creature melded with octopus fingers sticky with crud from their noses. I was a snake trapped inside buttery skin that just wouldn't molt, melt, molt, wouldn't let me go after so many years. The echoes of laughter sharp as a tanned hide stretched tighter over the mouth of an anxious drum before a night's performance puncture the ears of my brain. Then a shadow whiplashed across my forehead and I saw him, the eyes of one who understood, standing taller than a giant surveying the wretched waste where I lay. He stood like God with his wide shoulders and flapping long beard. I screamed, "Papa!" He brought a finger to his lips and hissed so low that my alimentary canal trembled its innards. It had been so long since he left us. I felt six years old again, my mother tugging my ear hard, telling me again and again I had to behave. She, the Monster of Mouth, devoured me every time I forgot a word in my Latin memorizations. She treated me like a carcass that didn't need a lot of feeding. I grew up hungry, hungry, starving mad for anything that would sustain me though woozy bouts of cold-eyed scummyness. Words, crumb-like, were a start. They slithered up and down my throbbing veins and exploded inside the globes of my eyes. I saw. There were no words to describe what I saw, but I saw. It was sky, moon, earth. Layers of false modesty cracked like walnuts. I saw the tripe squirm in the blank-eyed sun while vultures spun circles above. Then raggedy black wings, the puffy ascot, that terrible beak. I was hunger incarnate. I couldn't stop eating the meat of books to the spiny skeletons until they were dead in my hands. I had to leave Charleville. Paris didn't want me at first. But when Paul Verlaine invited me to come stay with him, I waltzed in and saw into his chest the heart of how much he'd longed to sex. I saw the wildness of drink and loneliness in his eyes, the unsaid dead eyes of his, until I showed him the vile gift between my legs. Filling him became my life in those iridescent days. Then came our little stabs of blood, mingling with the breathing of life back into the corpses of words, the itty-bitty skeletons discarded across the desert wasteland of the godforsaken page. We were worse than hydras with our many-tongued arguments shimmering amok on the paved streets of Paris and London. Everyday was a season of poverty, a season of plenty. We shouted and we drank and we laughed when I told him to go write filthy verse for the hell of it. By god, he friggin' did! But there in my eyes, straining to see, not like the days when I thought I saw the universe entire in a single glance, someone else:

the vast ship-shadow enveloping me, were his eyes of

stormy gray and the sails of his long beard, of hulls that

endured oceans and mad-eyed visions of land not seen

through the telescope, of soldier-sons he'd nurtured and

lost. He was distinctly American. This, I was sure. Then

I saw a flash of what he had once looked, younger and

arrogant with one hand on his hip and the other hand

reaching toward the center of himself inside his pocket.

A single tear as wide as a pond on a bright summer day

outside Pension Rossat splashed down on my being

entire. In the bleeding ocean of ash and electric jolts

frying the camel jelly of my brains, I drowned.

THE PRODIGAL BOAT
from Walt Whitman upon finding Arthur Rimbaud

You were a boat most impossible to steer,
but I was most alive when you were created.
I carved your hull out of the finest old-growth
wood from the deepest forests of lore.
Your varnished mast shone proudly in the sun.
I gave you tarp wings, and off you flew.
Your arrogant exuberance was understandable,
but age hasn't treated you well, my little boat.
You sailed across the black waters of Europe,
bumping into every ship the wrong way.
You leaked bile from all that absinthe.
Inhaling hashish made you lose track
of the stars overlooking every current.
Everything had to be done for a giggle.
You disappeared for shores far away
from here. You were given up for dead.
You've been breached. You're a ghost
haunting everyone who's ever seen you.
They've forgotten that you're not 20 anymore.
Come drop anchor here in the cradle of my arms.
My boy, let us grow old together in this madness.

WOMEN IN WHITE
after Walt Whitman

In the distance I saw her, a vision of white, sitting upright with her frilly white parasol and holding firm her reins on a huge black and mangy creature leaping forward up and down the dunes. I spat on my palms and rubbed them dry on my holey pants. It had been centuries since I'd sighted a lady. In the fading decades of my mortal existence on earth, I lied in my drivel about how superior the love of woman was.

I looked down on my young man, his eyes stricken with madness, writhe about on the smoking coals of sand. He knew I was there, but he'd lost the language to speak. The closer she approached me, the more I sighed relief. On her arm was a Red Cross badge. I watched the deep brown eyes of her oversized creature, a Newfoundland dog, never leaving mine as they came closer. He was as big as a horse! His lips dripped with drool. Before me he bent down like a camel and allowed the lady to slide off. She was in her fifties. Her eyes, fixing on mine, were brittle as iron. I knew who she was. She knew who I was. We'd never met, and we'd never read each other's work when we were mortally alive.

She didn't say a word as she whipped out a pillow for my young man's head, dipped a washcloth in ice water, and covered his face. His writhing stopped. She turned to me and held up a canteen. The tinny sound of water crashing waves inside was a symphony rescued from the attic of my life back in Brooklyn. I gulped greedily. She raised her hand that I had to stop. I nearly cried geysers of tears from so much gratitude. She took the washcloth off my young man's face and tilted his head to allow him to drink the last of her canteen.

As he drank, his eyes of sky gazed upward at mine of storms. There was an electric understanding, the same that I had with the young men I sighted for the first time. Their names were always inadequate for the words I wanted so much to express with my body. All this was pure language, older than time. He was as beautiful as any boy I had seen! I felt a wantonness rise up in my pants. She averted her eyes when she sensed my uneasy shift of weight from one foot to another. "I know why I never read you — *Indecent!*"

I gave a tight frown and a nod to show understanding. She pulled out a huge bowl and poured all of her second canteen. "Carlo — that great Beast — Bold as Nightingale — Stars stay aloof when He — Prances — My Heart a Wisp of Hair." I couldn't resist smiling as she and I watched Carlo bring every precious drop up to his cavernous mouth. She had spoken pretty much the same way she wrote. Her voice had a crisp authenticity. Me, I had to rewrite until I sounded like what everyone expected of me from having read my lines of lugubrious ecstasy.

She opened her parasol and stuck its handle in the sand next to the young man's head. The tensions in his face slackened until he looked ready to snicker. "*Est-ce que tu ne salis pas ta blouse blanche quand tu t'accroupis pour chier?"* She shot him a stern look. I didn't know French all that well, but there was no mistaking his demeanor. Her eyes squinty, she stood up and kicked the sand right into his face. He screamed, *"Va te faire foutre, sale gouine! Lesbienne! Gourmande des chattes! Tu es trop faible pour y résister. Ha!"*

She walked past me to Carlo, already down on his stomach and awaiting her to board. "What about your parasol?" We heard the sound of water tinkling. We both turned to him. I nearly gasped from laughter when I saw how he had leaned himself against the parasol handle and let loose. He pointed his middle finger at her. "Though not my Nature — Ill wishes — The Hand of God — Exceptions be made." He zipped himself up. *"Arrête de parler comme une bourgeoise. Parle normalement, comme nous cons!"*

Her eyes were hotter than the lava pits of Mount Vesuvius ready to spew atop Pompeii.

A silence. Then Carlo's ears perked up. We glanced about. What was that music? It was echoing from somewhere north. Carlo stood up and wagged his tail ever so slowly. Then came a vision floating along the currents of wind against the sea of sky: A black-haired woman with olive eyes draped in white stood high and mighty in a chariot burning wheels of smokeless fire while a quartet of white stallions galloped toward us. She held her lyre like a book and plucked the strings a song so simple it moved us closer. Her cheeks had the caked remnants of saline and sand.

"Sappho!" I called. We had met on the day I died. She was the one who introduced me to the first poets who appreciated my language of intimacies. If not for her, I'd have been still a lonely man wondering whether I belonged anywhere. It had been so long since we last saw each other. "You look as ravishing as ever! What brings you here?" She laughed when I leaned forward to kiss her perfectly formed hand. Her nails were like opal pearls. I stopped when we heard an outburst: "Angel that You are — Impossible — Spring's bloom Awakens — Hope that wings!"

She turned to that voice and seemed afraid to smile:

> *I heard the sound of a melody longing to be freed*
> *of its chains long covered with dust*
> *underneath your bed. I heard*
> *the drumbeat of your nervous heart,*
> *louder than the ticking of your father's clock.*
> *You gave up your life for him, never*
> *telling him how much you needed another*
> *heart to beat in time with yours*
> *and breast to breast. The song of loneliness*
> *is the most painful itch of all.*
> *I am nothing but melody*
> *full of the milk of aloe vera.*

THE LYRE

These carved arms hold firm
against strings that squirm.

I have tamed her notes.
I never play rote.

I have sung of love
and the gods above.

But you are a sight,
a woman in white

blazing still on ash,
a chariot dash.

Your hair is auburn.
To touch it I yearn.

My voice sails on wind.
You look as if sinned.

Has Zeus seduced you?
My heart fills with rue.

You were a maiden.
My heart feels laden.

Try again I must.
I've slept long in dust.

An ode I compose
of a lass who knows.

You break smiles so sly
like kites swaying high.

hums deep in my breast.
Your sweetest sound-chest

but lines I must keep.
My strings plucked will weep

Your words breathe in blood.
I become a flood.

Tears forever flow.
You still *care*. I know.

quill-inked strokes of spite.
Oh, your words are light,

so you can make art.
You must break my heart

Your darkness is tough.
I won't be enough.

will again turn blue.
In weeks or years: you

never locked to claim.
our chained tongues of flame

make love until dawn's still,
Under the stars we will

These here are just clothes.
Come, my love, come close.

fires my heart's dark maze.
The sun of your face

In the days when the Greek gods ruled the human universe, none was so evil and potent & the nine-headed serpent who guarded the underworld, the wonderland of the dead!

Millennia later, it has awakened.

Too many gods had run amok above, its slab of vibrating stalactite.

The groaning echoes of its wet body creeping
across the dunes of minced garlic ashes
sounding like a hiss, its nine heads
snarl while braiding its rubber giraffe necks.
In the distance it slithers like a hallucination,
tugging along a cape of thunder and lightning.

Its scales look like calligraphy stretched
in the blackest of ink against a black gray.
It pushes aside the shoulders of sand,
exposing the bedrock crypt of skeletons dead
of thirst and madness. Its weight sliding over
crumbles them into the smoky powder of coal.

The few ghosts remaining in the Sahara stand agape.
Centuries had inured them with impunity.
Walking through walls was their immortal right.
No one had warned them the nine heads undulating
could dance to bring back the eye-watering stench
of the very dead, the legends they'd cherished.

The first eight heads had unmasked the zombiefied faces
of their dead—daughter, brother, sister-in-law,
substitute son, mother, father, streetcar
conductor, and drunkard. The ninth head wagged
out a trio of tongues, lined
with crud and gravel and petroleum.

Its voice was deeper than cement cracking.
No words came out. Instead its thoughts swirled
like a tsunami around the few ghosts,
threatening to deafen them into submission.
They were not to write verse ever again,
or risk permanent imprisonment in the underworld.

As it rose higher like a cobra, enveloping them
into a shadow far colder than -73 Celsius,
the ghosts turned to each other. Their eyes,
filled with memory of love and ecstatic experience,
wept. They reached out and gripped each other's
hands. Songs much older than the first lyre arose.

Together they hummed and sang from the guts of marrow and memory:

a whisper of fear,

Darkness has come to claim
All that I can contain
My heart is a tiny flame
Lost in a hurricane

a kiss of awkwardness,

You are a book cover.
How should I open, read?
Confuse me more, lover.
Your eyes are all I need

a shout of joy and redemption,

Plankton that I am sails
Out the dark depths of home
My heart was tough as nails
Only to you I roam

a cry of agony

Veins like clotheslines stretched too
Far between us bleed red
Like eyes bruised black and blue
We might as well be dead

against the injustice of an unfeeling world:
together a soothing prayer of forgiveness.

However torn apart
Our limbs may take, may all
The heavens lend us heart
To absolve your spit's gall

The eight heads, rotting with grime and spit, leered
at their cute little voices. Slaying their eight muses
had been their finest hour, the cause of decay
that spread like cancer outward until it latched
onto the DNA code of greed and arrogance
until it replicated into the beautiful drought.

But the ninth head belonged to The Muse,
the loneliest creature known to exist. She longed
the friendship of anyone who would listen to her.
But nothing prepared her for the tender melodies
knifing through burps and belches of the other heads.
It had been so long since she'd heard such glorious music!

Without thinking, The Muse sank fangs deep
into the necks of her tormentors. The other
heads twisted and turned, trying to bite back
at The Muse. They chomped at each other
instead. The gaping holes they left behind
sprouted new heads far more repellant.

With each growth, the heads looked less and less
human. It was as if it was devolving back in time
when creatures didn't have limbs to twaddle
across the virgin shore after living in the sea
filled with plankton. Some of them didn't have eyes,
but their mouths stayed open and hungry.

They sniffed at each other and tore into the filets
embedded in each other's necks. But they didn't
have incisors deep enough to pierce. They wailed.
The Muse mustered enough strength to snap.
One by one, the eight fetusheads fell into the arms
of the ghosts. Their stilled faces were cradled.

The Muse collapsed from exhaustion. The powder of relief
turned into a dust storm gone in a minute.
The clouds stopped crackling. The air became cool.
The ghosts turned to the remaining living head
and looked quietly into her eyes as she breathed
her last. They bowed before the greatness of Her.

In the silence that followed, the ghosts kicked aside the ash until it was deep enough to bury the heads without elegies. They knew that to honor the love and the dead properly, they had to embrace the inky serpents slithering between the arterial vines of their deathly words.

FOR EMILY, LOST IN AMBER

Stuck in the goo of tree resin,
the Monarch butterfly struggles
to break free. It starves. More
tears of resin dribble around it.

So many Lost — Collected —
My herbariums — Labeled —
Plants of memory —

The pine tree collapses under
the groan of snow and slap of wind.
The tree and the butterfly lie together
in repose, their stories untold.

Caterpillars — Words of the page —
Awaiting Eyes — Springtime —
Cocoon opening —

The tree decomposed, the butterfly
withstands the velocities of time,
found after too many dust storms.
On the shelf, it stands a fierce hymn.

Books my Trees — Strong against Storms —
Knocked down — My lantern Cracked —
Seeds still Everywhere —

One day a new butterfly will emerge,
flexing her wings of stained glass.
The world will be her church.
Her faith will not crack this time.

FLICKERS

Together they dream fire: these women in white
standing in the desert's toxic sunlight.
The sky is a skeleton of clouds and ultraviolet holes.
It's still too hot to walk on bare soles.
The wheels of their chariot will take flight

burning high until gone from sight.
The women stay cool as night,
never baring to each other their souls.
Together they dream fire,

the kind that no one ever sees bright.
Their eyes flicker a twinkle so slight,
like panning for gold in bowls,
hoping for answers in the Dead Sea scrolls.
Nothing is ever black and white.
Together they dream fire.

ROUNDROCK ROAD
for J.T.S. and M.S.T. (in memoriam)

Growing up, he watched pixelated videos
squirreled away in YouTube's archives
of his ancestors carrying on
and laughing while the smoke curled
upward from the slabs of meat
on the grill. He'd longed for the day
when there was enough land
for buffalos and cows to graze
under a thicker ozone layer where no
one worried about the sun's toxic rays.

He'd spent his entire life never outside.
The air inside was slightly cool and stale,
drifting up and in through permeable glass,
a smoky screen of ashen tundra stretching.
When his father said he'd won a free trip
in a solarpod to travel anywhere in America,
he chose a city formerly known as Dallas,
Texas, when America was America.
They pored through pictures in the archives
and pinpointed the address on Roundrock.

That night he dreamed of the fabled
orchard of pecan trees blooming freely
in the backyard of long ago. His ancestors
had to give up that house—everything—in order
to migrate north, to the Yukon Biodome.
He wondered if the house had any books
left, made of paper, glue, and gloss,
shipwrecks lost in a sea of toppled shelves.
He'd seen horror documentaries of termites
and cockroaches mating and devouring.

In the solarpod he and Father sit
quietly. The hum of desert winds buffeting
their curved windows is loud,
distant. They coast, straight over free-
ways as an arrow zeroing on the red eye.
The landscape of sand and ash never vary.
The house of so many lost memories

has a broken shoulder, a gaping corner.
Armies of termites skitter, gathering
in the solarpod's hovering shadow.

Father and son step out, clad in white
anti-ultraviolet and termite-resistant
uniforms and moon boots. Winds,
having no humidity to weigh them down
like stones, whip about. The peltings
become white noise. The front door
already asunder, they entered the living
room, walls already cracked from incisors
tougher than diamond shards of hunger,
and spray pesticide into shadow puddles.

Father heads for an armoire leaning
sideways. He'd heard about the family
heirlooms of 19th century rifles and pistols
forgotten in the mad rush to leave decades
before. Son looks up the stairs. Up the steps,
he calculates each gasp from the shock of weight.
The railing is made of metal, a miracle.
Each dust-covered room reminded him of photographs
that had made him dream the mundanity of posters
hung on walls, real cotton sheets, and *books*.

But there aren't any books or paper anywhere.
In the hallway he looks up at the ceiling. There
is a tiny pull-down metal ladder. He pulls
a folding chair from the bedroom, pushing
against it to gauge the sturdiness of floor.
The ladder slides open with a squeaky groan,
its stretched tongue going *Ahhh*, its throat
the tiny esophagus to the lungs of a tiny attic.
The two-by-fours are rickety. The flash of
laser sears like a knife across the holey floor.

The periphery of shadow reveals a plastic box
half-melted. There are skeletons of books!
He kicks the box aside to scare the pulp-hungry
beasts. He peers inside. The books are pretty
much gone. But wait—a Penguin paperback hedged
between the flaps of a plastic children's book.
He pulls it out and holds it up to the light.

His pupils dilate at its cover of a bearded man
with long locks: *Leaves of Grass* by Walt Whitman.
Poetry? Ugh. But that doesn't matter!

He now owns a real book, made of hemp-free *paper*!
He unzips his breast lock, a dangerous
act in these parts, and slipped it in-
side his uniform. His heart beat faster
now that he had words on *paper* next to it.
How odd that no one had ever predicted
the contagious nature of modern incunabulum,
how people would die just for a touch
with something termites always ate for lunch.

Alone in his own room with lights dimmed,
he opens the Penguin book. He's never told anyone.
The opening essay about America bores him. He skips
Ahead to the first poem. He is startled by a sound,
listens again. Nothing. He resumes reading, then:
a tiny voice whispering. He glances about himself.
That's so strange! He doesn't look up when a voice
with a strange accent utters: "I celebrate myself..."
Every single word on a dead writer's page engraves
his eternal tombstone in the cemetery of obscurity.

THE ANNUNCIATION

The young man awakens to the sound of a lyre playing a simple song in the distance and the sight of a bearded shadow sitting in a chair next to him. "I've come to save poetry," the long-haired stranger says. "Will you help me?" The young man is stupefied to see the natural fibers and dark dyes in his shaggy clothes made centuries ago. Today clothes are made of recycled dye-free hemp.

The young man suddenly finds himself standing before a river that he has never seen before. It is just like in the wistful-eyed documentaries about the days when water was plentiful, except that he is truly *there*. The mist of cool water rising up coats him. It is a rare shiver, the kind that his drought-weary generation has always thirsted for. And so many tall evergreens! And so many birds flying! He'd never seen a wild bird fly with his own eyes. He turns to the wobbly old man leaning against a cane. "How did I get here?"

"Up here," the old man says while pointing to his temple, "and down here." He points to his heart. "And here." He thrusts out his crotch and grabs it. "Poetry's all three: brain, heart, and groin."

The young man steps back when he sees the river splashing and careening against the banks. "Why are you so afraid, my boy?" He sees salmon, once plentiful and wild but now farmed and coveted like the Beluga caviar, darting up and leap about in their mad rush upstream.

"Salmon," he whispers. "I've never seen them live before." He is more struck by the sight of corpulent tears streaming down across that thick bush of a beard and dripping like dew after a bright morning rain, and those wizened eyes staring at the waves rafting past. "Who are you?"

He snorts and taps his cane. "Does it matter? Life's a big mad raging river. Just dive in."

The young man reaches out, grabs at the fine bubbles of water, and licks his fingers. Water has never tasted this pure, so gluttonous. He looks down and sees the rich wet mud underneath him. He has never seen such a deep brown before. He squats down and scoops up a handful of virgin soil, an expensive rarity even in the bigger greenhouses. He inhales the musk of worms, the efficiency of ants, and the aroma of decayed leaves. Artificially manufactured smells could not compare to this! And the air! It didn't feel a reedy thin, but fresh, far fresher than the oxygen regurgitated inside the Yukon Biodome. He feels high from a single whiff. He closes his eyes, and the sun amazingly does not sear. The ozone layer must be thicker as in generations before.

He opens his eyes and finds himself squatting as before but in his room. The smell of all pungencies rising from the river is gone. His nose suddenly feels like weeping. He stands up and looks about in the dimness. The chair is still there. But there's a new distinct odor, the dust of time barely stitched together in a slim book with the cover embossed with the words *Leaves of Grass* set in a spidery leafy type. He feels a flare of recognition: He'd heard about the theft from the Yale Museum, its value already in the staggering millions.

He glances around his sparse room. A pair of gloves must be somewhere. He senses other presences in the room, but he can't pinpoint them.

A tap on the shoulder.

He whirls around and finds himself standing face to face with the man he now knows.

"My boy, forget about the gloves. You must live!" With that, the old man grabs the young man's hand, licks all of his five fingertips, and grabs the book off the chair. "Now I want you to *touch* the pages of this book the same way you *touch* yourself, lovingly, with unadorned passion. It's the only way to save poetry!"

As the centuries of dust and paper weigh ever so lightly in his hands, he looks up to find the old man gone. All that's left is a book. He raises the book up to his lips and begins licking each gold-leaf embossment until he feels golden with leaves of grass sprouting off the shores of that mighty river. Words from ghosts past are mere pathways to a sweet intoxicating madness enveloping like tendrils weaving around his tender root.

THE GYNOECIUM

from Ancient Greek: gene, *meaning* woman, *and* oikos; house

Venus and Aphrodite thus wedded:
Let us be less afraid of each other,
these strangely familiar curves
of our long-hidden bodies,
victim of too many doubt-filled winters
in the faces of men crawling everywhere,
these unfamiliar folds opening
like rose petals revealing pistils tipped
with passion-fruit nectar. Each sip
we tender each other is a dew drop
each morning after a night's rain
deep in the peat of our pillows,
entangling the waxy hair of dreams
among the squirming of worms.
Let us breathe dawn's heady oxygen,
circulate water in our veins,
and cling: such sweet caffeine!
Each day we will photosynthesize
the sun's brutal stares into softness,
the full greenery of mothering
the baby poems nestling among
our feet never leaving
but always wriggling toes,
itching for another kiss, another sigh.
Let us move together as one,
two flowers entwined in embrace
against the wind, awaiting
the blessing of bees spreading
the bloom of our new address.

THE FIRST TEAR

In the ocean of my gray eyes, I see ghosts
I should've known better while alive
evaporate. Had I just hallucinated,
or had I been blessed with divinities?
The Sahara's no place for worship.
I catch the shadow of you sharpening knives.

In the puddle of your blue eyes, I see skies
darkening. Your face turns overcast.
You open your mouth to speak. Out
comes spitfire and lightning. The first tear
dribbles off your face, the first rain-
drop of the Second Great Deluge to come purify.

My love, let's both drown together.
There's no finer death than resurrection.

. . . and so it begins.

ACKNOWLEDGMENTS

Among the Leaves: Queer Male Poets on the Midwestern Experience (Raymond Luczak, editor; Squares & Rebels): "The Gynoecium."

Ashé Journal: "Heresies" and "The Twelve Olympians."

Assaracus: "The Richness of Spit" and "Six Gallery, San Francisco: 7 October 1955."

Crab Orchard Review: "E-Signature."

Deaf Lit Extravaganza (John Lee Clark, editor; Handtype Press): "Silences."

Marginalia: "Creeping to the Shortest Day of the Year."

SIGNews: "Resuscitations."

We'll Never Have Paris: "Dehydration" and "Incunabulum."

Windy City Times Pride: "America's First Coming Out."

Wordgathering: "Hyperthermia."

An earlier version of this book was listed as a Finalist for the Sentence Book Award 2011. • The poem "Hyperthermia" won third place in the Inglis House Poetry Competition 2011. • The poem "How to Kill Poetry" was a response to John Lee Clark's poem "One Good Bad Way." • The poem "Roundrock Road" is in memory of James Thomas Sharer (24 September 1964 - 11 December 2007) and Michael Shannon Todd (11 December 1967 - 22 June 2011). • The quotes used in the poem "Ms. Monroe's Rebuttals" come from Harriet Monroe's autobiography *A Poet's Life: 70 Years in a Changing World* (Macmillan, New York, 1938).

The author wishes to thank Bryan Borland, John Brennan, John Lee Clark, David Cummer, Mitch Gould, Stephen Kuusisto, Michael Olson, Anthony Santos, Tom Steele, Michael Shannon Todd (*in memoriam*), and Phillip Ward for their assistance with this book. T.A. provided the French translations for the poem "Women in White."

IMAGE CREDITS

Except where noted, all public domain (PD) images were sourced from Wikimedia. Mona Z. Kraculdy created all photo compositions for the cover and the "Leaves of Glass" section.

Dedication Page || Watercolor Etching "Ancient of Days": William Blake.

Front Cover || TOP: Arthur Rimbaud: Etienne Carjat • Walt Whitman: Matthew Brady (courtesy of the Library of Congress) • Desert Scene: Edward Musiak • BOTTOM: Emily Dickinson: William C. North • Lily: Raymond Luczak • Photograph "First Snow": Kees Smans (keessmans.com).

Spine || *The Domesday Book.*

Back Cover || FIRST ROW: Sappho: "Prioryman" • Homer: PD • *Beowulf* Excerpt: Kip Wheeler • Johannes Gutenberg: PD • William Shakespeare: PD • Phillis Wheatley: Scipio Moorhead • Lord Byron: Thomas Philipps • SECOND ROW: Henry Wadsworth Longfellow: Julia Margaret Cameron • Harriet Monroe: Eva Watson-Schütze • Gwendolyn Brooks: "MDCArchives" • Allen Ginsberg: Michiel Hendryckx • Sylvia Plath: Wellesley High School graduation photo (1950) • Clayton Valli: Unknown (courtesy of Gallaudet University Archives) • BACKGROUND ART: Photograph "Edifice of Erosion": Von Glitschka • BOTTOM: Raymond Luczak: Self-portrait.

Section Covers || FRONTISPIECE: Chrysanthemum: Raymond Luczak • THUS SPAKE ZARATHUSTRA: Photograph "Creation of Adam" by Michelangelo: "1a2b3c" • THE WARMTH OF WINTER: Photograph "Naked" by Wes Peck • LEAVES OF GLASS: Photograph "Erato": "ChrisO" • Photograph "AntiqueDirtyPaperTexture_05": Dustin Schmieding (valleysinthevinyl.com) • ENDPIECE: "The Birth of Venus" by William-Adolphe Bouguereau.

Inside Section Covers || Graphic "Spray_Paint_5": Daniel Davidson (sadmonkeydesign. com).

ABOUT THE AUTHOR

Raymond Luczak is the author and editor of 15 books, including the poetry collections *Road Work Ahead* (Sibling Rivalry Press), *Mute* (A Midsummer Night's Press), and *This Way to the Acorns* (Handtype Press). His prose titles include *Assembly Required: Notes from a Deaf Gay Life* (RID Press) and *Men with Their Hands: A Novel* (Queer Mojo), which won first place in the Project: QueerLit 2006 Contest. He has edited a few anthologies, most notably *Among the Leaves: Queer Male Poets on the Midwestern Experience* (Squares & Rebels) and *Eyes of Desire 2: A Deaf GLBT Reader* (Handtype Press). He is the editor of *Jonathan*, a journal of short fiction by gay, bisexual, and transgender men.

Born and raised as the only one deaf in a family of nine children in Michigan's Upper Peninsula, he lost much of his hearing at the age of eight months due to a bout of double pneumonia and high fever, but this was not detected until he was two and half years old. From that point on, he wore hearing aids and learned to speak. He was not allowed to use sign language until he was 14. After graduating from Houghton High School in 1984, Luczak moved to Washington, D.C. to attend Gallaudet University, the world's only liberal arts university for the Deaf. There, he learned American Sign Language (ASL) and came out as a gay man. After participating in the Deaf President Now movement with his Class of '88, he graduated with a B.A. in English. A few months later he moved to New York City where he would live for the next 17 years. He soon scored a national breakthrough with his essay "Notes of a Deaf Gay Writer" on the cover of *Christopher Street* magazine. A few years later his first book, *Eyes of Desire: A Deaf Gay & Lesbian Reader* (Alyson), won two Lambda Literary Award nominations (Best Lesbian and Gay Anthology, and Best Small Press Book).

As a storyteller, Luczak has had many lives. One of them is that of a playwright with 19 plays performed in three countries. His first full-length effort, *Snooty: A Comedy*, won first place in New York Deaf Theater's 1990 Sam Edwards Deaf Playwrights Competition. In addition to having the play performed three times since 1996, it is included in his drama collection *Whispers of a Savage Sort and Other Plays about the Deaf Experience* (Gallaudet University Press).

As a filmmaker, he directed the full-length documentaries *Guy Wonder: Stories & Artwork* and *Nathie: No Hand-Me-Downs*. He worked with the renowned ASL storyteller Manny Hernandez on *Manny ASL: Stories in American Sign Language*. Luczak regularly posts clips of his poems translated into ASL and subtitled in English on YouTube.

In 2005, he moved to Minneapolis, Minnesota where he is constantly trying out new recipes while his terrier mix Rocky proves to be an excellent sniffer in the kitchen.

raymondluczak.com

ABOUT SIBLING RIVALRY PRESS

Founded in 2010, Sibling Rivalry Press is an independent publishing house based in Alexander, Arkansas. Our mission is to develop, promote, and market underground artistic talent—those who don't quite fit into the mainstream. We are proud to be the home to *Assaracus*, the world's only print journal of gay male poetry, and *Jonathan*, a journal of fiction by gay male writers. Our titles have been honored by the American Library Association through inclusion on its annual "Over the Rainbow" list of recommended LGBT reading and by *Library Journal*, who named *Assaracus* as a best new magazine of 2011. While we champion our LGBTIQ authors and artists, we are an inclusive publishing house and welcome all authors, artists, and readers regardless of sexual orientation or identity.

siblingrivalrypress.com

"Re-vision—the act of looking back, of seeing with fresh eyes, of entering an old text from a new critical direction—is for woman more than a chapter in cultural history: it is an act of survival. Until we understand the assumptions in which we are drenched we cannot know ourselves. And this drive to self-knowledge, for women, is more than a search for identity: it is part of our refusal of the self-destructiveness of male-dominated society."

— Adrienne Rich